CONTENTS

Michael Herbert is hereby identified as author of this work in accordance with
Section 77 of the Copyright, Designs and Patents Act 1988

YORK PRESS
322 Old Brompton Road, London SW5 9JH

PEARSON EDUCATION LIMITED
Edinburgh Gate, Harlow,
Essex CM20 2JE, United Kingdom
Associated companies, branches and representatives throughout the world

First published 2000
Third impression 2007

ISBN: 978-0-582-42459-3

Designed by Vicki Pacey
Phototypeset by Gem Graphics, Trenance, Mawgan Porth, Cornwall
Colour reproduction and film output by Spectrum Colour
Produced by Pearson Education Asia Limited, Hong Kong

PART ONE

INTRODUCTION

HOW TO STUDY A POEM

Studying on your own requires self-discipline and a carefully thought-out work plan in order to be effective.

- Poetry is the most challenging kind of literary writing. In your first reading you may well not understand what the poem is about. Don't jump too swiftly to any conclusions about the poem's meaning.
- Read the poem many times, and including out loud. After the second or third reading, write down any features you find interesting or unusual.
- What is the poem's tone of voice? What is the poem's mood?
- Does the poem have an argument? Is it descriptive?
- Is the poet writing in his or her own voice? Might he or she be using a persona or mask?
- Is there anything special about the kind of language the poet has chosen? Which words stand out? Why?
- What elements are repeated? Consider alliteration, assonance, rhyme, rhythm, metaphor and ideas.
- What might the poem's images suggest or symbolise?
- What might be significant about the way the poem is arranged in lines? Is there a regular pattern of lines? Does the grammar coincide with the ending of the lines or does it 'run over'? What is the effect of this?
- Do not consider the poem in isolation. Can you compare and contrast the poem with any other work by the same poet or with any other poem that deals with the same theme?
- What do you think the poem is about?
- Every argument you make about the poem must be backed up with details and quotations that explore its language and organisation.
- Always express your ideas in your own words.

This York Note offers an introduction to the *Selected Poems* of T. S. Eliot and cannot substitute for reading of the text.

T.S. Eliot is one of the greatest modern poets. His poetry *demands* to be read by anyone who has an interest in the poetry of the twentieth century, and the best place to start is with the poems that Eliot himself chose to make up his *Selected Poems*, first published in 1954, containing work first published between 1915 and 1934. You may then wish to move on to the later *Four Quartets* (1943), or his verse dramas such as *Murder in the Cathedral* (1935), and all students will benefit from the study of Eliot's criticism, which ranks equally with the poetry as a major contribution to twentieth-century literary culture: the theoretical counterpart of his poetic practice, it provides insights for the poetry, as well as being valuable in its own right. But the study of the *Selected Poems* on its own is a perfectly possible and valid activity, and it is the obvious and sensible place to begin any exploration of probably the leading **Modernist** poet. The first poem in the book, 'The Love Song of J. Alfred Prufrock' (1915), has been described by the American poet John Berryman as the first modern poem, and its centrepiece, *The Waste Land* (1922), is widely regarded as the greatest poem of the twentieth century: certainly, it is hard to think of any other poem that has a stronger claim to that accolade.

Eliot, then, is one of those poets who are generally acknowledged as major and central. But, though his name is well known, his poetry is less so: it has a reputation (not undeserved) for being difficult, which puts many potential readers off, while others who make a brave start on it can soon find themselves lost, and are discouraged from continuing. These readers need guidance, of the kind this Note aims to provide, with the hope that, once some of the difficulties are cleared up and insight gained into Eliot's subjects and styles, his audience can better savour the peculiar pleasures he has to offer. Among these pleasures are shock and surprise, sometimes involving startling juxtapositions and often involving humour, but also the recognition of unusual beauty and psychological truthfulness to experience. Eliot's vision of the modern world has become one of the 'givens' of literary culture, and his poetic voice is one of the most distinctive of all: therefore, as students of the poetry of the twentieth century, we can arguably have no more rewarding challenge than to try to see that unique vision and hear that unique voice. This Note attempts to clarify and illuminate the vision, and help in learning to listen to the voice.

Those things that make Eliot's poems uniquely deserving study, and those that make it difficult, tend to be much the same. The most obvious may be summed up in the phrase 'oddity and obscurity'. This is a rather rough and ready label, but, though limited, it is not false or misleading: on the contrary, it is a general truth about Eliot that his work is unusual and hard to understand.

Eliot seems odd or strange in both style and subject matter to those whose idea of poetry is derived from, say, a **Romantic** poet such as Wordsworth. Just as Wordsworth, reacting against eighteenth-century ideas of literary decorum, introduced beggars or village idiots into his verse and was attacked for it, so Eliot in his turn was castigated for his 'dirty gutters' or 'cigarettes'. Just as Wordsworth tried to describe everyday events in everyday language, so Eliot is not afraid to use language and situations so ordinary that many readers miss the special, extraordinary effects he creates:

> I grow old ... I grow old ...
> I shall wear the bottoms of my trousers rolled.
> ('The Love Song of J. Alfred Prufrock', 1915)

That is both comic and tragic, both touchingly pitiful (**pathos**) and deliberately falling, in an **anticlimax**, from the serious to the ridiculous (**bathos**). Such combinations make it difficult for us as readers to know how to react. Should we laugh or cry, or both, or what? Eliot himself keeps well hidden behind his highly cultivated ironic tone, by which he can appear to be doing one thing (perhaps serious) and yet can undermine it by a hint of something else (perhaps humorous) in the words he chooses, or present a character in two opposed lights; it is typical of his method to lighten his pessimistic views by comical verbal antics, and startle us by the striking placing together of apparently unrelated phrases.

In that last instance, obscurity begins to mingle with oddity. The fragmentary, apparently incoherent jumble of unconnected ideas, often stemming from the poet's compression of several concepts into a compact new image-combination, may not only look very peculiar on the page –

> For Thine is
> Life is
> For Thine is the ('The Hollow Men', 1925)

– but may also seem so obscure as to elude the understanding of even experienced readers. Sometimes, too, Eliot's **symbols** can cause difficulty: when they are not generally accepted symbols (as the Cross is a symbol referring to a whole cluster of ideas called Christianity) but ones the poet has evolved himself, the reader can have problems understanding to what concepts they refer. The value of such symbols, however, is that they can go beyond narrow reference to be widely suggestive, opening up a broad range of ideas and feelings. Whereas the Garden of Eden, for instance, is an archetypal symbol for lost innocence, gardens in Eliot's poetry can either symbolise experiences which have never been had, which have been missed rather than lost, or beauties which have to be renounced – just as their flowers are almost always among Eliot's symbols of frustrated sexual desire. Similarly, Eliot's frequent lack of a normal logical order in his poetry can go beyond a merely narrative progression to provide striking juxtapositions and accumulations of suggestive images, making use of repeated words and themes and patterns in a manner closer to the sequences of music than the statement of facts in plain prose. But of course any unusual combinations of words, any omissions of expected linking phrases, any puzzling symbols make things harder for readers anxious to know 'the meaning' of a poem.

Another difficulty is Eliot's notorious use of allusions and quotations. Some of these refer to well-known historical events, works of literature, and so on. Others refer to more obscure sources; and the erudite or learned nature of these can be a further problem, especially when written in foreign languages. There is no agreement among critics as to how far a knowledge of Eliot's sources is necessary for a reading of a particular poem, and how far such knowledge is irrelevant. If readers miss certain allusions, they may miss some of the point of a poem: perhaps a resonance or cross-reference, perhaps a quotation that evokes the original context as a contrast to its present context. This brief Note cannot track down all Eliot's allusions, but even the selected allusions to which attention is drawn may cause unnecessary anxiety. The main thing is not to let your reading of the poems get bogged down in sources and references: these can be followed up later, if you are interested.

Faced with Eliot's fragments, his unusual subjects and styles, his allusions and other difficulties – in short, his general oddity and obscurity – we as readers have to work at his poetry to get much out of it, rather than sitting passively letting it wash over us as can some pleasant poetry. We can aim to *accept* the oddities by making them familiar enough not to worry us by their unusualness, without losing their surprise value – one of the great pleasures Eliot can give. We can aim at making *apprehensible* the obscurities by clearing up as much of the difficulty as we can, without letting remaining puzzles stop our developing response to the poems as poetry. Only then will we be in a position to make an *assessment* of the value of this poetry for us. In all these areas, this Note is intended to offer a stimulus: it may not have all the answers, but it should provoke you into at least asking some fruitful questions about Eliot's *Selected Poems*.

PART TWO

COMMENTARIES

Selected Poems, a selection of his poetry made by Eliot himself, was first published by Faber and Faber in 1954. The first paperback edition, published in 1961, has been reprinted regularly ever since, and is the edition used in this Note. This section of the Note deals with all the poems in the selection, and in the same order.

PRUFROCK AND OTHER OBSERVATIONS (1917)

The dedication of this first volume of Eliot's poems records the death, in the Dardanelles campaign of the First World War, of Jean Verdenal. He was an intimate friend Eliot made during his year in Paris in 1910–11. In the quotation from Dante (*Purgatory* XXI, 133–6) the power of such friendship is described by Statius (*c.*AD45–96), one of Virgil's imitators, who stoops to touch his master's feet in homage, forgetting that they are both bodiless spirits: 'Now can you understand the measure of love that burns in me for you, so that I forget our vanity, and treat the shadows as solid things'. In contrast, the poems in this volume, from which Eliot has chosen four, present futile, sordid lives, lacking satisfying friendships.

THE LOVE SONG OF J. ALFRED PRUFROCK

Prufrock ponders the nature of his existence

The poem dramatises the state of mind of Prufrock, a tragi-comic figure of uncertain age. He is very much in the mould of the Laforguian (see Allusions in Critical Approaches) self-mocking little man, by his own account physically unimpressive and sexually timid, cultured and sensitive. In his painfully self-conscious **monologue** he imagines going through sordid streets to the room where the women chatter, but coming away having failed to achieve anything: though this is his 'Love Song', he cannot make a declaration of love. Nor dare he do or say anything else of any significance (his 'overwhelming question' suggests not merely a proposal of marriage, but a larger question as to the meaning of life), he is so unheroic, so self-conscious, and so shy of communicating with any of the women, whom he seems to despise as well as fear. From them he turns to a fantasy of love with mermaids until real voices call him back to the stifling real world.

The title neatly undermines the romantic associations of 'Love Song' by the ridiculous name, not forgetting its self-important initial 'J.', while suggestions of prudishness may be combined with 'Proof-rock' as a punning variant of 'Touchstone'; for Prufrock is both primly proper and a test case for the reader's reactions. Incidentally, the name is not entirely whimsical: young Eliot signed himself T. Stearns Eliot; Prufrock was the name of a furniture dealer in St Louis.

As always in Eliot, the **epigraph** is also significant in various ways. For instance, there is the parallel of a tormented sufferer in a personal hell; the implication of the reader as a fellow-inhabitant of Prufrock's hopeless world; a suggestion that one part of Prufrock (timid and thinking) is deluding another (passionate and feeling), turning him to fraudulent fantasy rather than true engagement with life.

The 'you' of the first line seems to be the reader at first, but 'you and I' could be two aspects of Prufrock – his thinking self addressing his public personality – though the final 'we' that drowns may not be only the whole Prufrock, but a universalising touch. Elsewhere 'you' is the equivalent of 'one', or can even be addressed to one of the women, and so on. The opening **similes**, likening the evening to a patient under anaesthetic and the streets to stages in a wearisome argument, and the **metaphor** comparing the fog to a lazing cat, tell us more about Prufrock's mental state (especially his morbidity and inertia) than the objects they are ostensibly describing. This use of images to characterise moods and feelings continues throughout: look, for example, at the coffee-spoons and cigarette-ends that sum up Prufrock's dull days, or the way he (equally pathetically) pictures himself as an insect stuck on a pin, or a crab deep in the sea. The final sea imagery of escape seems suddenly liberating after all the images of feebleness and futility that culminate in trivia about eating and dressing, but reality quickly reasserts itself, drowning Prufrock, not in the fantasy sea, but in the social world in which he flounders.

The words of the **epigraph** (or motto), again a quotation from Dante (*Hell* XXVII, 61–6), are spoken by the most famous warrior of his day, Count Guido da Montefeltro (d. 1298), in Hell for false advice to Pope Boniface (d. 1303), from a flame that trembles when the damned speak: 'If I thought my reply would be to one who would ever return to the world, this flame would shake no more; but as no one ever returns alive from this depth, if what I hear is true, I answer you without fear of disgrace'.

And indeed there will be time this and the following twenty-five lines echo the words of the Old Testament preacher in Ecclesiastes 3:1–8: 'A time to be born, and a time to die; … A time to kill, and a time to heal'

works and days the title of a poem by the Greek writer Hesiod (eighth century BC)

a dying fall Duke Orsino's description of a piece of music in Shakespeare's *Twelfth Night* I.1.4

wept and fasted, wept and prayed a biblical imitation, in both the a-b-a-c form of the repetition (as in Psalm 118: 'Thou art my God, and I will praise thee: thou art my God, I will exalt thee') and the vocabulary (as in 2 Samuel 12:22: 'I fasted and wept')

my head brought in upon a platter as was the head of the prophet John the Baptist, cut off by order of King Herod at the request of Salome as a reward for her dancing (Matthew 14:3–11)

the eternal Footman apparently a personification of death, made socially suggestive, this recalls the 'Heavenly Footman' in the allegorical *Pilgrim's Progress* (1678) of John Bunyan (1628–88)

squeezed the universe into a ball / To roll recalls 'To His Coy Mistress', by Andrew Marvell (1621–78), in which the poet urges his mistress to immediate, passionate love: 'Let us roll all our strength, and all / Our sweetness, up into one ball'

Lazarus (a) the dead man whom Christ raised to life again (John 11:1–44); (b) the poor man sent to Heaven, whom Dives, a rich man in Hell, asks to be sent back from the dead to make the living repent (see Luke 16:19–31)

tell you all as Christ promised the Holy Ghost would 'teach you all things'
(John 14:26)
sprinkled streets sprinkled with sawdust, as in the Boston Eliot knew while
at Harvard
Prince Hamlet Shakespeare's Hamlet; like Prufrock in his self-awareness
and worry about being indecisive (the line-ending echoes Hamlet's 'To be or
not to be' soliloquy), but unlike him in heroic stature. Prufrock goes on (in
imitation Elizabethan style) to liken himself, instead, to Polonius, the
talkative, moralising old courtier in *Hamlet*; or even the court jester (the
Fool)
Full of high sentence description of the learned and elevated talk of the
Clerk in *The Canterbury Tales* of Geoffrey Chaucer (1340?–1400)
bottoms of my trousers rolled turned-up trouser-ends were then becoming
fashionable
part my hair behind again the latest fashion
mermaids singing recalls 'Teach me to hear mermaids singing', in a 'Song'
by John Donne (1572–1631), as well as contrasting with the sirens of
Greek legend, whose singing led sailors to drown, and with the calling to his
human wife of 'The Forsaken Merman', a poem by Matthew Arnold
(1822–88)

PORTRAIT OF A LADY

A younger man describes an affected romantic lady

A hostess is here seen through the eyes of a younger man, who quotes her
words and describes her effect on him during the three visits presented in
the poem's three sections. By his own poses, the narrator reveals things
about himself. In each section of his **monologue** he is satirical about her
rarefied pretensions and repeated desire for friendship, which frightens
him off. But finally he wonders, as he imagines her death, if he is right to
feel so; if perhaps her finer feelings, though pathetic and affected,
triumph over the trivia of his own life.

The title, in recalling that of *The Portrait of a Lady* (1881), a
novel by Henry James (1843–1916), draws attention to Jamesian
influences on Eliot at this time. Just as the situation and
mannerisms in 'Prufrock' may have been partly suggested by
James's story 'Crapy Cornelia' (1909), in which a self-conscious

ageing bachelor visits a younger widow but never puts the 'important question' (a proposal of marriage), so the closely-related 'Portrait' is also very Jamesian, as in its use of a central consciousness (the young man) to describe the ostensible main subject (the lady); in its subtle discriminations and ironies; in its presentation of those who shrink from life; even in the mannerisms of the lady's speech – though her original was the Miss Moffat who gave elegant tea-parties for Harvard undergraduates.

The **epigraph** helps to focus the criticism of the narrator: the 'sin' he has committed is that he is uncommitted, though humane enough to allow doubts about his lack of involvement to creep in later. There is also the link between the somewhat callously treated deaths of abandoned 'wench' and abandoned 'lady'.

Eliot's favoured seasonal imagery distinguishes the sections: as in Prufrock's October, smoke and fog and descending darkness mark the late months of the outer sections, set against the spring flowers (lilacs and hyacinths) and sunsets of the middle section. But the sections share a musical imagery that fits in with the lady's romanticism, from the satirically-treated Chopin concert and the thin violins and distant cornets echoing the delicate conversation (while the narrator gets a drumming in his head as his own 'prelude'), through the violin and street piano serving as uneasy reminders, to the 'dying fall' of the lady's persistent music. She, ridiculed for the affectations of her drawing-room (the candles, the conversation, the clutter), repeats the word 'friend(s)' a dozen times, clings to youth and twists the lilacs in an image of frustrated sexuality, the sadness and monotony of her life caught also in the repetition of the line about sitting and serving tea. He, however, twice wishes to escape and smoke a cigarette, and does effect an escape on the central occasion when he is embarrassed by her confession. For his frequent smiles, whether patronising or pained, can be wiped out by her openness; just as, though he may be going abroad (leaving the 'another country' of the epigraph) and could forget her, he imagines her memories will pursue him to worry him about his own feelings and reactions.

For further discussion, see Text 1 of Extended Commentaries.

epigraph from *The Jew of Malta* (IV.1.41–4), a play by Christopher Marlowe (1564–93)

Juliet the ill-fated young heroine of Shakespeare's romantic tragedy, *Romeo and Juliet* – an ironic contrast with the ill-fated 'affair' of Eliot's lady and young man

Preludes piano pieces by the romantic Polish composer Frederic Chopin (1810–49)

two or three echoes the words of the resurrected Christ, 'Where two or three are gathered there am I' (Matthew 18:20)

cauchemar (*French*) nightmare

My buried life 'The Buried Life', a poem by Matthew Arnold, speaks of the feelings we often suppress

I take my hat in order to depart

'dying fall' see notes to 'Prufrock' above

PRELUDES

A series of pictures of modern city life

The first two Preludes present evening and morning, stressing the smells and general sordidness of the street scene, the last two a woman and a man, both suffering inwardly from their perception of their miserable lives of squalor and routine, their respective visions of the street in the morning and evening. Finally, the poet speaks in his own person to sympathise – then everything is dismissed by a laugh; the universe is indifferent.

The title suggests a musical analogy, mood pictures on the same theme, developing by repetition and variation. The images create a general impression of squalidness (almost every noun and adjective has an unpleasant connotation), weariness and repetitiveness (mirrored by all the repeated words). As in 'Prufrock', personality becomes limited to attributes and to parts of the body such as feet and hands.

Some of the details are derived from the novels of low life in Paris by Charles-Louis Philippe (1874–1909), whose *Bubu de Montparnasse* includes the sordid morning awakening of a woman in the slums. Other suggestions are developed in a critical way from certain beliefs of the French philosopher Henri Bergson (1859–1941), including his idea of the soul being formed by the memory of images projected on to the passive mind as by a film: Eliot's own technique has been seen as 'cinematic', a series of images flashing on to the mind. Both Philippe and Bergson also influenced the following poem.

shades window-blinds
papers from your hair for making the hair curl

RHAPSODY ON A WINDY NIGHT

A nocturnal ramble

Between the hours of midnight and four in the morning the narrator wanders the streets, each thing he sees by the light of the street-lamps awakening memories. Finally he reaches the everyday objects of home, which, by inviting him to the routine of life, make a final cruel irony, as he has just seen 'life' to be empty and unpleasant, marked by assorted unattractive sights and smells.

The title again has musical connotations, suggesting an irregular composition of a rather wild kind. But the images that bring alive the poet's memory at the different times are not entirely random. Some are sinister: the prostitute with the skew eye who evokes other crooked images; the moon as a feeble-minded woman. Some are unthinking: the cat, the child, the crab. Some are decayed or dead: the geraniums (twice), the branch and broken spring, the moon again. And so on, until a mood of disorder, futility and deadness pervades everything.

lunar synthesis made one by moonlight
Dissolve the floors of memory an idea from Bergson (see 'Preludes' above) of images pouring randomly into the memory to join together
madman shakes a dead geranium a combination typical of the French Symbolist poet Jules Laforgue (1860–87)
Remark the cat ... child's eye 'Le Joujou du Pauvre', a prose-poem by another French Symbolist, Charles Baudelaire (1821–67), about a poor

child's toy (a rat), includes the cat eating scraps. Notice Eliot's French
constructions: 'Regard ... Remark ...'

La lune ... rancune 'The moon harbours no ill-feelings': a wittier version of a
line of Laforgue's in *'Complainte de cette Bonne Lune'*; Laforgue's moon
imagery has influenced Eliot's in this poem

chestnuts ... female smells also linked in *Marie Donadieu*, another novel by
Philippe (see 'Preludes' above), whose *Bubu de Montparnasse* also provided
details in this poem, such as the woman in the doorway and the awareness
of smells

Poems 1920

Apart from 'Gerontion', the poems in this section are all written in
regular stanzas of four lines each, with four beats to the line, and rhyming
a-b-c-b (except for 'The Hippopotamus'). T.S. Eliot and Ezra Pound at
this stage felt that **free verse** had gone too far towards looseness, and
proposed as a remedy a strict form adapted from the **quatrains** of the
French writer Théophile Gautier (1811–72) in his *Émaux et Camées*
(*Enamels and Cameos*). Then Eliot moved on again to 'Gerontion', which
was originally to be part of *The Waste Land*.

Gerontion

The meditative monologue of an old man

This poem again presents a state of mind: that of an old man meditating
on (a) the personal loss of feeling and meaning in his own dried-up,
unheroic life; and (b) the more general decay of humanity through
religious and historical decadence. Despite this bleak vision, he does not
totally despair: everything is not totally purposeless, nor are the inevitable
cycles of nature stopped.

The title brings to mind other literary old men, as in 'The Dream
of Gerontius' (1866) by Cardinal Newman (1801–90), a vision of
Heaven rather more optimistic than Gerontion's; but Eliot's
diminutive form makes his *little* old man deliberately pathetic,
like an older Prufrock. As the **epigraph** taken from Shakespeare's

Measure For Measure indicates, his voice is that of another shrinker from life, a life not fully lived. In the same speech from which the quotation comes, the Duke of Vienna, disguised as a friar, advises the young Claudio (about to be executed) to 'be absolute for death' because life holds little, and old age has 'neither heat, affection, limb, nor beauty'; Gerontion lacks all these but is not 'absolute' for life or death, just hanging feebly between them.

The sections of the poem are linked in various ways, some simple – the use of repeated words like 'old man', 'dry', 'wind', and so on – and some more difficult to grasp. The poem is difficult chiefly because of the *fusions* it creates.

Firstly, there is a fusion of individual humans and humanity. Gerontion is an old man and any old man. Mr Silvero and the other sinister sounding foreigners in that section are specific representatives of the general decline of religion (see below). Similarly, the international sounding De Bailhache, Fresca, and Mrs Cammel, individual damned sinners, stand for all: ingenuity might even stretch to identifying the first sinner with fighting anger (French suggestions of axe or bailey); the second with amorous lust (as in the Fresca in the drafts of *The Waste Land* and Dante's Francesca in *Hell* V); and the third with the avarice of the rich (a camelhair coat is a sign of wealth, and Christ said it is easier for a camel to pass through the eye of a needle than for a rich man to enter Heaven).

Secondly, there is a fusion of present and past. Gerontion's mind shifts continually between his present situation and his past memories. His very name recalls the ancient past, as does the war reference to Thermopylae; but modern events are also part of history, hence the references to present (1919) events at the end of the First World War. Gerontion also worries about the decay of religion from Christ to the present debasements, the whisper of devotion now offered to decadent gods: Mr Silvero (silver = money?) worships his valuable porcelains; Hakagawa (as in Japanese, could *haka* = tomb, *gawa* = take the side of?) worships dead artists; Madame de Tornquist (does her name suggest something torn, tattered and twisted?) is holding some kind of spiritual séance, perhaps a Black Mass (the candles as on an altar), with Fraulein von Kulp (Latin *culpa* = guilt?) apparently a guilty accomplice or client.

Thirdly, the meanings of words fuse. Allusions to past literature fuse with modernity in passages that particularly imitate the **blank verse** of Jacobean dramatists. The words themselves, by deliberate ambiguities, strikingly fuse Gerontion's frustration in the face of the confusions of history and the decadence of religion with his sexual frustration: for example, the passage about the frustrations of history could just as easily apply to a woman, and the whole poem is full of words that have a sexual connotation – from the warm rain for which sterile Gerontion longs, through the rented house that may be a brothel, the biblical 'knowledge' and the suggestions of vice (and the 'kept' woman and adultery, in one line), to those ambiguous features of the physical universe, the shuddering Bear, the Horn, the Gulf, even the Trades (as in Shakespeare, echoes of the trade of bawd or prostitute).

By such means every significant idea in the poem dissolves into another. It is a technique that was also to be used in *The Waste Land*.

Gerontion (*Greek*) little old man
epigraph slightly misquoted from Shakespeare's *Measure for Measure* (III.1.32–4)
Here I am ... for rain Eliot derived these first two lines almost word for word from A.C. Benson's biography, *Edward FitzGerald* (1905), together with other details in the poem such as the woman in the kitchen
hot gates a direct translation of the Greek Thermopylae, a pass in Greece, the scene of a great battle with the Persians (480BC)
the Jew squats the first unflattering portrayal of Jews in *Selected Poems*: there are others in the next poem, in 'A Cooking Egg' and in 'Sweeney Among the Nightingales'
estaminet (*French, of Belgian origin*) small café
merds (*from the French, 'merde'*) dung, excrement
Signs ... wonders a quotation from a sermon preached by Bishop Lancelot Andrewes (1555–1626) on Christmas Day 1618 on the text Luke 2:12–14 (the Angel tells the shepherds of the birth of Christ, swaddled in a manger)

'We would see a sign!' the cry to Christ of the unbelievers who wanted a miracle (Matthew 12:38)

The word ... with darkness derived from the same sermon by Andrewes: 'the Word without a word; the eternal Word not able to speak a word ... swaddled ... with the swaddling bands of darkness' (the last six words taken from Job 38:9). For the association of Christ and the Word, see the opening of St John's Gospel

juvescence Eliot's alteration of 'juvenescence' refers through Latin to the 'joyful', 'young' time of year, spring

Christ the tiger recalls 'The Tiger', a poem by William Blake (1757–1827), contrasting God's creation of this fierce beast and the gentle lamb – a more usual **symbol** for Christ: as Andrewes says, 'Christ is no wild-cat' (Christmas sermon of 1622)

In depraved ... judas each detail of this line comes from the opening paragraph of Chapter 18 in *The Education of Henry Adams* (1918), where Adams (1838–1918) describes the lush spring in Maryland. Eliot's selection of detail stresses the 'depravity': May is too beautiful to be good; red-blossoming dogwood could be menacing or, with the chestnut, sexual; the judas tree recalls the betrayer of Christ

To be eaten ... drunk as are Christ's body and blood in the bread and wine of Holy Communion

Mr. Silvero for this and other characters, see analysis above

Limoges a town in France, noted for its porcelain

among the Titians a phrase in Chapter 7 of Henry James's novel *The Wings of the Dove* (1902), describing Milly Theale at the National Gallery in London among paintings by the great Venetian artist Titian (1487?–1576)

Vacant shuttles ... the wind compresses into an image of futility the complaint of Job in the Bible that his days 'are swifter than a weaver's shuttle, and are spent without hope ... my life is wind' (Job 7:6–7); 'The void awaits surely all them that weave the wind' is a passage appearing in the first chapter (which was already published) of James Joyce's famous novel *Ulysses* (1922)

contrived corridors brings not only general deception and complication but also the particular Polish Corridor to mind – a strip of land taken from Germany by the Treaty of Versailles in the year (1919) Eliot wrote this poem

wrath-bearing tree particularly suggests 'the tree of the knowledge of good and evil' (See Genesis 2:17), which brought God's anger when Adam and Eve ate its forbidden fruit

concitation (*from the Latin*) rousing up, excitement

I that was near ... therefrom recalls a line in *The Changeling*, a play by Thomas Middleton (1580–1627): 'I that am of your blood was taken from you' (V.3.151)

inquisition the religious overtones hint at the Inquisition, a body set up by the Roman Catholic Church to seek out and punish heretics

multiply ... mirrors by increasing the number of images and angles seen, as Sir Epicure says in *The Alchemist*, a comedy by Ben Jonson (1572–1637): 'my glasses / Cut in more subtle angles, to disperse/ And multiply the figures, as I walk / Naked between my *succubae* [concubines]' (II.2.45–8). There may also be a further link with the Hall of Mirrors in which the Treaty was signed at Versailles

whirled ... Bear the idea that the damned are carried away, after death, into space (the Great Bear is a constellation), as in the classical imagery of these lines from *Bussy D'Ambois*, a tragedy by George Chapman (1572?–1634) that Eliot gave as his source: 'those that suffer / Beneath the chariot of the snowy Bear' (V.4.105–6)

fractured atoms the atom was first split in 1919

Belle Isle a small island in the straits between Newfoundland and Labrador

Horn Cape Horn, southern tip of South America

Gulf Gulf Stream (ocean current)

Trades trade winds

BURBANK WITH A BAEDEKER: BLEISTEIN WITH A CIGAR

A jaundiced view of tourists in Venice

Decline from past to present is here portrayed in an impression of Venice, visited by contrasted tourists, the sensitive Burbank set against the second appearance of Eliot's repulsive Jews. After falling for a sexual adventuress, soft Burbank loses out to hard cash (Bleistein then Klein) and is left with his thoughts.

From the very large number of allusions (most of them to Venice) in this short poem, one can see what fun Eliot has had in taking his allusive technique so far. The guidebook in the title gives the clue,

and in the **epigraph** we find a guidebook-type potted history of
Venice in literature, mixing the serious and the trivial, the great
and the decayed, the noble and the depraved. Sexual depravity
is prominent in the poem, as expected in the city famed for
its courtesans ('Princess' Volupine is evidently one such) and
notorious in Shakespeare's day as the 'best flesh-shambles' in Italy.
Shakespeare's Venetian money-lender, Shylock, obviously assisted
Eliot's presentation of the international Jewish businessmen (Sir
Ferdinand Klein anticipates Sir Alfred Mond in 'A Cooking Egg')
who succeed where poor cultivated Burbank does not: even the
ignorant, ape-like Bleistein, with his rich man's phallic cigar, seems
to have better luck than the impotent idealist.

Burbank Eliot may be recalling the American botanist Luther Burbank
(1849–1926)

Baedeker a once-popular guidebook series, known for its compact entries
with historical and other information for tourists

Bleistein German name (meaning Leadstone) of a Jewish fur-dealer in
London that Eliot may have noticed there

Tra ... laire adapted from the second of Gautier's 'Variations on the Carnival
of Venice' in *Enamels and Cameos* (1852)

nil ... fumus 'nothing but the divine lasts; the rest is smoke' – written
round a smoky candle in a painting of martyred St Sebastian by Eliot's
favourite artist, Andrea Mantegna (1431–1506), in Venice (Palazzo della
Ca d'Oro)

the gondola ... pink from the first chapter of *The Aspern Papers* (1888), a
Venetian story by Henry James

goats and monkeys in Shakespeare's *Othello* (IV.1.263), the 'Moor of
Venice' names traditionally lustful animals in his rage against his wife
Desdemona and her supposed lover

with such hair too! from 'A Toccata of Galuppi's', a poem of decay and
death by Robert Browning (1812–89), invoking the Venetian composer
Baldassare Galuppi (1706–84)

so the countess ... departed these closing words of *The Entertainment of
Alice, Dowager Countess of Derby,* by John Marston (1575?–1634), are the
only ones in the epigraph without a clear connection with Venice: perhaps
Eliot's joke here is to direct the reader to the Venetian play by Marston

quoted in the third stanza, or even to his Venetian *The Insatiate Countess* –
a more likely counterpart to the insatiable Princess Volupine
a little bridge perhaps a smaller 'Bridge of Sighs', over which Venetian
prisoners went to execution, as Burbank to his 'fall'
Descending at a small hotel another obscure joke may connect Burbank with
two civilised Americans, Henry Adams and Henry James, who, as Eliot had
recently written (*The Athenaeum*, 23 May 1919), arrive in Europe and
'descend at the same hotel'
Volupine this name combines the voluptuous with the wolfish (lupine) and
foxy (vulpine); compare also Ben Jonson's Venetian comedy of the grasping
Volpone, or The Fox (1606)
They were together, and he fell a comic reversal of a line from 'The Sisters'
('They ... she fell' – seduced by an earl), a poem by Alfred, Lord Tennyson
(1809–92)
Defunctive music funeral music; a phrase used by Shakespeare in 'The
Phoenix and the Turtle', for 'Love and constancy is dead' (as Burbank
discovers)
passing bell rung at a person's death
God Hercules in Shakespeare's *Antony and Cleopatra* strange music shows
that 'the God Hercules, whom Antony lov'd, / Now leaves him' (IV.3.21–2)
because he has abandoned the military life of a Roman leader for the love
of Cleopatra; once again an exotic seductress brings about a man's downfall
horses which draw the chariot (hence 'axletree') of the Sun, as depicted on
the bronze doors of St Mark's Cathedral, Venice, or in Marston's Venetian
play, *Antonio's Revenge* (1.1.107–8): 'the dapple grey coursers of the morn
/ Beat up the light with their bright silver hooves'
Istria peninsula east of Venice
shuttered so that her doings cannot be seen, as well as shading from the
sun
barge / Burned recalls Shakespeare's description in *Antony and Cleopatra* of
Cleopatra's barge that 'Burn'd on the water' (II.2.202)
protozoic slime where the lowest forms of life began. Protozoa are
microscopic animals consisting of a single cell
Canaletto a painter (1697–1768) famed for his pictures of the canals of
Venice
On the Rialto a phrase used more than once by Shylock the Jew in
Shakespeare's *The Merchant of Venice*, referring to the building in Venice

BURBANK WITH A BAEDEKER continued

where business deals were made. Eliot continues the traditional associations
of Jews with money (and the fur trade in the following lines)
Lights, lights twice in Shakespeare (*Hamlet* III.2.264; *Othello* I.1.142)
lights are called for on occasions of apparent treachery and sexual
misdemeanour; hence the relevance to Princess Volupine's infidelity
Klein literally 'small' (another German name)
clipped the lion's wings a winged lion is the emblem of St Mark and Venice.
A link with 'Time's ruins' is suggested by a line by Jonathan Swift
(1667–1745) in the introduction to *A Tale of a Tub*, where hack writers
who have 'clipped his wings, pared his nails, filed his teeth' triumph over
Time; see also the opening of Shakespeare's Sonnet 19: 'Devouring Time,
blunt thou the lion's paws'
meditating ... ruins recalls 'To meditate amongst decay, and stand / A ruin
amidst ruins', from *Childe Harold's Pilgrimage* (IV, xxv) by Lord Byron
(1788–1824), concluding Byron's lament for once-great Venice
seven laws presumably the seven principles of architecture of John Ruskin
(1819–1900), whose *The Stones of Venice* describes the decline of
Venetian Gothic architecture

Sweeney erect

Sweeney in a brothel

A grandly inflated opening, with classical references to desertions in the
heroic past, degenerates into a sordid modern affair in a brothel ('the
ladies of the corridor' and 'the house' seem euphemistic), with Sweeney
callously shaving while the woman left in the bed, a nameless epileptic,
has a fit. The madam, Mrs Turner, and her 'ladies', are indignant for their
reputation; but one sensibly brings restoratives.

The caricature Jew of the two previous poems is now replaced
by the caricature Irishman, and a stagey exaggeration marks the
poem from the deliberately overwrought classical setting to the
grotesque modern contrast in the horrid portrayal of Sweeney
and the unfortunate woman whose epilepsy parallels a violent
sexual encounter with an apeman. He, despite the sinister razor,
seems milder after he has pompously (and mock-Emersonianly)
'addressed' himself to shave, all fat and pink and unconcerned, a

would-be man-of-the-world who thinks he understands women; and the tone changes to fit the lighter satire on the selfish concern of Mrs Turner and her ladies, till the 'But' suggests some praise for practical Doris at least.

Sweeney recalls Sweeney Todd, the demon barber of Soho who, as created in the 1840s for a melodrama (though reputedly based on fact) by T.P. Prest, cut his victims' throats while shaving them. Eliot seems to have based his character on an Irishman who taught him boxing at Harvard. Sweeney is the archetypal Irish 'Wild Man', as in the twelfth-century Middle Irish poem, *The Frenzy of Sweeney*

Erect this humorously combines a sexual significance with a human definition of the apelike Sweeney as *homo erectus,* upright man – earlier than *homo sapiens,* modern 'wise' man. It also hints at an ironic reversal of the view of man held by Ralph Waldo Emerson (1803–82), as in his essay 'Self-Reliance', where independent man 'stands in the erect position ... works miracles' – a view that Eliot's portrayal of Sweeney will undermine

epigraph from *The Maid's Tragedy* (II.ii.74–7) by Francis Beaumont (1584–1616) and John Fletcher (1579–1625): the broken-hearted Aspatia, who has lost Amintor, tells her maids to model their needlework picture of Ariadne, who lost Theseus, on herself, and to make the background appropriately miserable. The poem then takes up these instructions

Cyclades ring of Greek islands in the Aegean, subject to winds and earthquakes (with new islands appearing, as in 1570 and 1770)

anfractuous twisting, winding, contorted

Aeolus Greek god of winds

Ariadne in Greek myth, this daughter of King Minos of Crete loved the Athenian Theseus and gave him string to help him get out of the Cretan labyrinth, into which he went to kill the Minotaur, her monstrous half-brother; but later Theseus abandoned her on the Cycladic island of Naxos

perjured sails if he successfully killed the Minotaur, Theseus was to change the black sails with which he set out; but he forgot, and his father, Aegeus, misled by the 'lying' sails, threw himself into the sea that was then named after him

Nausicaa in the *Odyssey* of Homer, this princess helps Odysseus the morning after he is shipwrecked on her island; though eager for marriage to him, but not wishing to appear a man-hunter, she and her father, Alcinous, remove all obstacles to his return home

Polypheme Odysseus escapes from the cave of man-eating Polyphemus, leader of a race of one-eyed giants, the Cyclopes, by blinding him while he sleeps, and hiding away among the sheep let out in the morning to graze

orang-outang apeman Sweeney will later also suggest 'The Murders in the Rue Morgue', a story by Edgar Allan Poe (1809–49) in which the murders occur after an orang-outang takes its master's razor, lathers its own face in front of a looking-glass, and attempts to shave

root of knots another reversal of Emerson, who in his essay 'History' grandly calls man 'a knot of roots, whose flower and fruitage is the world' – a superior being quite unlike Eliot's monstrous creation

The lengthened ... said Emerson in 'Self-Reliance', Emerson states that 'An institution is the lengthened shadow of one man ... and all history resolves itself very easily into the biography of a few stout and earnest persons': Eliot telescopes these views

sal volatile ... brandy these restoratives may also be a concluding bathetic link between the sordid modern episode and Ariadne, who in one version of her story is found (abandoned in Naxos) by Dionysus, the god associated with wine, who revives and marries her

A cooking egg

The narrator revisits a female acquaintance

Yet another meditation on time's decay, with the narrator, following hints that he is a fairly 'bad' fellow, revisiting a childhood acquaintance (apparently now a prim spinster) and feeling final regret and sorrow after the humorous list of his needs to be fulfilled by others in Heaven.

This elusive little poem has been given much attention by those anxious to identify the 'Cooking Egg' and the owner of the child- and bird-like name (nickname?) Pipit, who has been variously described as a young girl and the visitor's elderly former nurse. After noting the nature of such an egg, together with the real 'bad egg' of the **epigraph**, and seeing what details about Pipit are hinted at in the poem (how proper she is, her 'distance' from the 'I', her spinsterly-seeming knitting, her sentimental Victorian possessions, her limited experience, the past link shown by the shared treat), the reader is best advised to follow the changes of tone from section to section: the rather sour amusement at the mixture of dignity and **pathos** in Pipit's situation; the comic whimsicality of the heavenly fancies, mockingly juxtaposing past and present; the serious final vision, regretting past losses and sorrowing over the tragic present. Once again it is the nature of the **monologue** itself, the nature of the mind here poetically dramatised, that is the real interest of the poem.

title an egg not fresh enough to be eaten on its own, if not yet entirely bad
epigraph the opening lines of the *Testament* of Francois Villon (1431–63 or later), looking back at his past sins: 'In the thirtieth year of my age / When I had drunk up all my shame'
sate an old-fashioned form of 'sat' for old-fashioned Pipit
Invitation to the Dance suggests a sentimentally philistine taste in the arts, whether it is a picture or a piece of music
Sir Philip Sidney (1554–86), the heroic Elizabethan, an epitome of honour
Coriolanus this general became the proud hero of Shakespeare's last Roman play
Sir Alfred Mond (1868–1930), Jewish capitalist, a founder of Imperial Chemical Industries
lapt (*archaic*) wrapped
Exchequer Bond a British bond issued by the government at 5 per cent interest
Lucretia Borgia (1480–1519), a member of a powerful and notorious Italian family; several times married, she would certainly provide both 'Society' and entertainment
Madame Blavatsky (1831–91), a Russian spiritualist, a founder of the Theosophical Society
Sacred Trances an occult secret of Theosophy
Piccarda de Donati Dante (*Paradiso* III) is taught by this nun, forced to break her vows, at the lowest level of Heaven
But where ... Where ...? Eliot imitates the classical Latin rhetorical trick (*Ubi sunt ...?*) of asking regretfully about past memories, a technique used in Villon's *Testament* (see epigraph)
penny world a trade expression for a cheap range of cakes and sweets
behind the screen where children ate in Victorian dining-rooms

Kentish Town and Golder's Green North London suburbs
eagles ... Alps evidently a reference to a failed Roman military expedition
(the legions carried an eagle emblem)
A.B.C.'s London cafés owned by the Aerated Bread Company

THE HIPPOPOTAMUS

The hippopotamus is compared with the Church

The poem sets up a satirical contrast between the 'merely flesh and blood' hippo who goes to Heaven and the indolent, rich, self-righteous, greedy, stagnant and ignorant 'True Church' left below on earth.

This earliest of Eliot's **quatrain** poems shares the title of a poem by Gautier, and is the only one to use Gautier's full a-b-a-b **rhyme**-scheme; but where Gautier in 'L'Hippopotame' likens himself to the hippo in fearless freedom, Eliot's animal is made, in a comical paradox, 'weak and frail' as any mortal flesh – yet (as with all sinners) standing a better chance of salvation than the self-satisfied Church. There is savage humour in the direct contrast between the lowly hippo and the grand capitalised Church in six of the nine stanzas, and at the end, after initial ironic acknowledgement of the superiority of the Church over the 'frail' hippo has given way to the hippo's heavenly reception, a venomous final unironic attack on the befogged institution.

epigraph St Paul, writing here in his Epistle to the Colossians (4:16), urges that his words encouraging the faith of these early Christians should be sent on to the Laodiceans, who are described elsewhere in the Bible (Revelation 3:16–17) as 'lukewarm' believers who say 'I am rich ... and have need of nothing' – rather like Eliot's complacent Church
rock Christ's pun on the name of St Peter and petra (*Greek* = rock): 'thou art Peter, and upon this rock I will build my church' (Matthew 16:18)
God works ... way adapted from a hymn by William Cowper (1731–1800), 'God moves in a mysterious way / His wonders to perform'
quiring in a choir (*archaic*, quire)
Blood of the Lamb the blood of Christ, the Lamb of God, sacrificed for the sins of the chosen who have 'washed their robes, and made them white in the blood of the Lamb' (Revelation 7:14)

miasmal mist poisonous gas from rotting matter, which suggests a decaying Church smothered in the fog of error; Elizabeth Barrett Browning (1806–61) uses 'miasmal fog' in her poem *Aurora Leigh* (vii.717)

WHISPERS OF IMMORTALITY

A meditation on death and sex

The Jacobean attitude of Webster and Donne in linking death and sex is set against a modern separation: sex is restricted to a temptress called Grishkin, with her well-fleshed body, our metaphysical ('beyond the physical') ideas restricted to death, with its fleshless skeletons.

The change of style at mid-point, from morbid Jacobean gravity to colloquial lightness, emphasises the contrast between the two halves, though the 'dry ribs' that keep modern metaphysics going are effectively placed at the end to tie up with the 'breastless' skeletons at the beginning as well as Grishkin's welcoming bosom. Eliot is here poetically elaborating – in the loss of the seventeenth-century simultaneous apprehension of death-in-life, mind-and-body – one of his related critical beliefs, the 'dissociation of sensibility' (from his essay 'The Metaphysical Poets'): that whereas Donne and his fellows combine thought and feeling and 'feel their thought as immediately as the odour of a rose', later writers have lost this connective power.

title a fainter version of Wordsworth's 'Intimations of Immortality'
Webster (1580?–1625?), a dramatist noted for sensational imagery, much concerned with sex and death, in violent plots
Daffodil ... eyes! in Webster's tragedy *The White Devil* (V.4.135) there is 'A dead man's skull beneath the roots of flowers'
pneumatic bliss a joke derived from two aspects of a Greek word meaning 'of the spirit' or 'of wind', and so with associations both sacred (spiritual) and profane (as in a pneumatic drill)
Abstract Entities the joke here is that sexy Grishkin draws round her even the philosophers who deal in such abstract ideas of reality
Circumambulate walk round as if shy of engaging

MR. ELIOT'S SUNDAY MORNING SERVICE

Impressions of the Church from theologians through painters to the laity

This satire on the Church has three main points: it uses paradoxically neuter agents of reproduction to show how the Word of God (Christ) multiplies in the many words of the biblical commentators; it contrasts with these the painter's one simple and lasting image of the Trinity; and it attacks a Church that can make a living out of people from whom it seems remote.

The learnedness of this ecclesiastical extravaganza must, despite the humour, frighten off more readers than it ever entertains, but is appropriate to the subject. There is Eliot's characteristic use of sexual images to present mental and spiritual states, and further links are provided throughout the poem by, for instance, pictures (the window panes may show a troop of divines in stained glass as well as the bees; there is the central religious painting; and there is the suggestion of another painting in the angel-supported gateway to Purgatory in the sixth stanza) and word play (the last word looks back to the first monstrosity). The final introduction of Sweeney gives a shock when we are expecting 'Mr Eliot': shifting in his bath he grotesquely parodies both baptism and the shifts of the scholars, yet without any application to such ordinary mortals the whole theological debate is meaningless, as meaningless as the obscure words would be to such people (if not Mr Eliot). By an appropriate contrast, Sweeney and the painting in the third and fourth stanzas are much more easily understood.

epigraph as in 'Portrait of a Lady', from Marlowe's *The Jew of Malta* (IV.1.22); here the Jew's servant sees two friars, 'caterpillars' who feed off society
Polyphiloprogenitive wanting many offspring; Eliot added a 'poly' (= many) to a word used in the 1865 English translation of *A New Life of Jesus* (II.41) by David Friedrich Strauss (1808–74), relating God, in the mystery of the begetting of Jesus, to the 'philoprogenitive Gods of the heathen'
sapient sutlers the (would-be) wise sellers of provisions to an army, in this case the learned scholars who provide the Lord's soldiers with arguments about the Bible

In the beginning was the Word Christ as the Word; the opening of St John's
Gospel, which continues 'and the Word was God'
Superfetation multiple fertilisation (and hence multiple births) of 'the One'
(*Greek*) – nicely illustrated by the preceding identical repetition
mensual turn (due) month
enervate Origen this seminal Christian theologian (*c.*185–*c.*254) was
believed to have castrated himself, the better to father a reputed 6,000
religious books; his teachings, particularly on the problematical relationship
of Christ, God the Son, to God the Father, in turn produced numerous
controversies
Umbrian school Italian school of painting, at its peak in the fifteenth
century under the leadership of Perugino (*c.*1450–1523)
gesso ground plaster surface prepared for a wall painting
Baptized God Christ was baptised by John the Baptist in the River Jordan –
a popular subject in Western art, with the other two Persons of the Trinity
usually looking down from above
Paraclete the Comforter, or God the Holy Ghost (represented in painting as
a dove)
sable presbyters black-clothed; elders of the Church (Origen was an
ordained presbyter)
piaculative penitential (Eliot's own coinage from 'piacular'); by payment
('pence') for their probably sexual sins, the repentant, pimply young
churchgoers hope to earn forgiveness
invisible and dim a phrase from 'The Night', by the devout poet Henry
Vaughan (1622–95)
bees linked with the sutlers as fertilising agents
epicene neuter, with characteristics of both sexes or no sexual
characteristic, as are – despite their fertilising function – Origen and the
worker bees

SWEENEY AMONG THE NIGHTINGALES

Sweeney is threatened in an unsavoury setting

Ape-like Sweeney is here relaxing in some low den, where two females
are thought to be plotting against him, and tension mounts as the other
men draw away from him – then the poem sweeps on to recall a classical
murder, the death of Agamemnon.

SWEENEY AMONG THE NIGHTINGALES continued

This dramatic poem advances in a remarkable series of shifts. The low-key opening immediately gives way to that 'sense of foreboding' that Eliot once said was all he consciously set out to create in the poem. For a while the spectacle of the fallen woman in the cape and the staring man in brown lift the tension, but as the thirty-two lines of the long final sentence gather momentum, the details become ominous and threatening: the man in brown's withdrawal; the accomplice's murderousness; the departure (and reappearance at the window, with his sinister gold-toothed smile) of the man who has rejected an advance; the distant host talking to a dark figure. Before anything happens to Sweeney, the eternal nightingales prelude the sombre grandeur of that ancient murder.

In all, a striking conclusion to the 1920 volume, with power rising above puzzle.

For further discussion, see Text 2 of Extended Commentaries.

title this recalls Elizabeth Barrett Browning's 'Bianca Among the Nightingales', a poem in which nightingales 'sing through death', as they do at the end of Eliot's poem; 'nightingales' is also a slang term for prostitutes, among whom Sweeney is placed in the poem

epigraph 'Alas, I am struck deep with a mortal blow': from the *Agamemnon* (line 1343) of the Greek tragedian Aeschylus (525–456BC), the cry of King Agamemnon as he is murdered by his adulterous wife, plotting with her lover

maculate spotted (as a giraffe, and implying the sinfully spotted who are not 'immaculate')

circles ... moon circles round the moon foretell storms

River Plate or Plata, in South America; its name implies the riches expected in its hinterland

Raven a constellation; this bird proverbially forebodes death

hornèd gate true dreams, in classical mythology, pass from the underworld through a gate of horn to get to man, false ones through a gate of ivory

Orion ... Dog the constellation of Orion (the Hunter) includes the Dog Star (Sirius)

man in mocha brown may be a returned First World War soldier in khaki, as Agamemnon was a returned hero from the Trojan War

Rachel *née* Rabinovitch another of Eliot's nasty Jews
nightingales ... bloody wood Eliot said he was thinking of the grove of the
Furies at Colonus: 'I called it "bloody" because of the blood of Agamemnon
in Argos'; in *Oedipus at Colonus* by Sophocles (495–406BC) this grove is
filled with nightingales that sing as Oedipus goes to his death, and in the
Agamemnon Aeschylus uses the image of the betrayed nightingale in a
prophecy of death
the Sacred Heart of Christ, stressing his suffering for humanity
liquid siftings of excrement

THE WASTE LAND (1922)

This work was cut down from a much larger one with the help of Eliot's
friend Ezra Pound (1885–1972), 'the better craftsman' (*il miglior fabbro*)
of the dedication; the original drafts were published by Eliot's widow in
1971 (Faber and Faber). It is also a work built up from a number of
separate poems, a manner of composition found again in the next two
poems, *The Hollow Men* and *Ash-Wednesday*, which may account for
some of the apparent discrepancies and dislocations between the sections
of all three works that can cause local difficulties of interpretation, but the
shared **metrical**, tonal and emotional characteristics of the sequences
weld each into a coherent poetic unity – and it is grasping that overall
effect, rather than puzzling over isolated uncertainties, at which the
newcomer to such poems should aim.

Perhaps 'coherent' hardly seems the right word to use of *The Waste
Land*, made up as it famously is from apparently jumbled fragments, but
even that description indicates a unifying feature: a fragmented vision of
the fragmented modern world is in fact characteristic and typical of the
poem, giving it a homogeneity through its very heterogeneity. Increasing
study reveals that the parts are related not only through such shared
stylistic features, but also through cross-references, and a definite (if not
always very obvious) development through the poem.

This development is not the usual development of a linear narrative:
there is no narrator, no single speaking voice, and no 'story' or 'plot' to
follow through, which has left many readers stranded. Rather than
thinking in terms of narrative, or even a looser version of the kind of

poetry that is more obviously thematically and stylistically organised, it is more useful to think in terms of other arts than literature. Think of the poem progressing with the logic of *music*, with repetition and variation of motifs; or as built up like a *collage* in art, where bus tickets and such odds and ends may be stuck onto the canvas in varied juxtapositions; or as operating like a *film*, in which the picture can (for example) cut suddenly to a different scene or point of view, or dissolve, or move in from a large-scale panoramic sweep to an intimate close-up. All these techniques are used in *The Waste Land*, and you should be on the lookout for them – and others – as you read.

The title phrase is used by Thomas Malory (*c.*1400–*c.*1471) in Book 17, Chapter 3 of his *Morte d'Arthur*, a work that, in describing the quest for the Holy Grail, relates to the work by Jessie L. Weston on the Grail legend that Eliot refers to in his Notes on *The Waste Land*. (These are printed on pp. 68–74 of *Selected Poems*, and are not duplicated in the notes that follow below unless further clarification seems necessary.) Mentioned twice in Eliot's Notes, but only hinted at in the poem itself, is the Fisher King, who, as described by Jessie Weston, links the search for the Grail to the restoration of the waste land: this sexually damaged ruler of an infertile land waits for the finding of the Grail to bring regeneration.

The **epigraph** is from the *Satyricon* of the Roman writer Petronius (1st century AD): 'For with my own eyes I saw the Sibyl of Cumae hanging in a bottle, and when the boys said to her: *Sibyl, what do you want?* she replied: *I want to die.*'

I THE BURIAL OF THE DEAD

Death and the living dead

After the awakening of April in 'the dead land' is seen as cruel after winter cosily buried us in oblivion, Marie speaks of herself, and particularly her memories, especially one of which she was frightened. Fear returns in a biblical response to the fragmented futility in the desert of modern life, then a German lyric about an absent love precedes emotional memories about 'the hyacinth girl'. Death is prominent in the subsequent fortune-telling by Madame Sosostris and the vision of the dead in London.

The abrupt changes of perspective in this opening part are a good preparation for the rest of the poem and a good illustration of Eliot's non-narrative technique. Despite all the dislocation, however, there are plenty of strong links in the four verse-paragraphs, of which death and fear are only two of the most obvious. Spring reviving memories and desire, for example, is taken up in the memories of Marie and the hyacinth girl, and the speaker recalling the latter is linked to both German quotations (see below) from *Tristan and Isolde*, the opera by Richard Wagner (1813–83): the sentiments of the lovelorn sailor in the preceding quotation and, in his paralysed half-life, the 'waste and empty' sentiment of the succeeding quotation. Apart from such links within the opening part, there are links with later parts: for instance, 'the drowned Phoenician Sailor' and 'death by water' reappear as drowned Phlebas in the fourth part, 'Death by Water' . See if you can find other such links.

title   from the Book of Common Prayer

Starnbergersee   lake near Munich, a holiday resort

Hofgarten   public park in Munich

Bin gar ... deutsch   (*German*) 'I'm not Russian, I come from Lithuania, pure German', said to Eliot by Countess Marie Larisch, whose reminiscences in *My Past* (1913) are used in this section

Marie   see previous note

broken images   see Ezekiel 6:6: 'your images shall be broken'

a handful of dust   from the fourth Meditation of *Devotions upon Emergent Occasions* (1624) by John Donne (1572–1631)

Frisch ... du?   (*German*) 'The wind blows freshly to the homeland. My Irish child, where are you waiting?'

Oed' ... Meer   (*German*) 'Waste and empty is the sea'

Madame Sosostris   borrowed from Madame Sesostris, the fake fortune-teller in Chapter 27 of *Crome Yellow* (1921), a novel by Aldous Huxley (1894–1963)

Those are ... eyes   from Shakespeare's *The Tempest*, I.2.401 (also at line 125)

Belladonna   (a) 'beautiful woman' (*Italian*); (b) a poisonous plant

the Lady of the Rocks   cf. the famous painting by Leonardo da Vinci, *The Virgin of the Rocks*

I THE BURIAL OF THE DEAD continued

Stetson though Eliot denied this, perhaps referring to Pound, who wore
such a cowboy hat
Mylae sea battle between the Romans and Carthaginians, 260BC
Dog ... friend in the dirge in *The White Devil*, to which Eliot refers in his
notes, this reads 'wolf ... foe' (V.4.103)
hypocrite ... frère (*French*) 'hypocrite reader, my fellow-man, my brother'

II A GAME OF CHESS

Two contrasted scenes and empty relationships

An absurdly inflated and therefore **mock-heroic** setting of the first scene
preludes the lack of communication between a neurotic woman and a
taciturn, gloomy man. The other scene, set in a pub, has a female
Cockney tell the sordid, loveless story of Albert and Lil, who is worn
out by childbearing.

The references to unfortunate historical and literary sexual
encounters in the title and text (see notes below) help give a
universal context to the two unhappy relationships then presented,
with a further universalising touch in the fact that the first
relationship is from a higher, better-educated class than the second,
yet both are equally marked by chasms between the partners:
clearly, Eliot thinks that the unhappy side of sex is unaffected
by differences of time, place or class. There is certainly no happy
side, here or elsewhere: does this suggest a certain limitedness in
his view of sexual relationships?

title at the repeat of this phrase at line 137, Eliot's note refers to the game
of chess in *Woman Beware Woman*, a play by Thomas Middleton
(1580–1627), where the moves in the game correspond to the seduction of
a young woman (II.2)
The Chair ... throne the echo of Shakespeare's *Antony and Cleopatra* (noted
by Eliot) is part of a highly seductive presentation of the Egyptian Queen,
other details of which filter into subsequent lines
laquearia panelled ceiling; Eliot's note quotes from the description of the
banquet given by Queen Dido for Aeneas, who later abandons her
Philomel ... forced she was raped by King Tereus and turned into a
nightingale (see also lines 205–6)

Y

'Jug Jug' Elizabethan imitation of (a) the nightingale's song; (b) sexual intercourse (also line 204)

Shakespeherian Rag from a ragtime hit of 1912, 'That Shakesperian Rag, / Most intelligent, very elegant'

Hurry ... time called by the bartender at closing time

Good night ... night love-maddened Ophelia's words in *Hamlet* IV.5.72

III THE FIRE SERMON

Many examples of lust

Nature is polluted, ugly death everywhere, and the repeated refrain from Spenser's idyllic wedding song contrasts with the series of examples of sordid sex: Sweeney and the prostitutes, the rape by Tereus (again), Mr Eugenides's offer of a dirty weekend, the unfeeling encounter between the typist and the clerk 'seen' by Tiresias and contrasted with the seduction of Goldsmith's Olivia, Queen Elizabeth and the Earl of Leicester, the violations of three daughters of London, the lusts of young St Augustine.

The series of examples of casual, violent, mechanical, unaffectionate or just lustful sex are framed by references – in the title and at the end – to the sermon preached by Buddha against the burning fires of consuming passions like lust. But there is also much water and particularly river imagery to unite the whole. This series packs the first paragraph: it starts with the opening image of the river in winter, without its leafy tent of overhanging trees, continues through Spenser's refrain and the modern Thames, Lake Leman, fishing in the canal, the shipwreck from *The Tempest*, and concludes with the Porters' soda water. The following sections have the oblique reference to the freight of the Smyrna merchant and the sailor home from sea, and water returns in the quotation from *The Tempest* in line 257 and the 'fishmen' of line 263, before the song of Wagner's Rhine-maidens is interwoven with references to the Thames, as Elizabeth and Leicester advance their love on the river, and, of the three 'Thames-daughters', one loses her virginity in a canoe and one at the seaside. Can you identify the water imagery in the rest of the poem? (It is found in each of the five parts.) Does

its function vary? You could similarly look over the whole poem
for repeated images of (for example) rock and stone, desert, broken
things, bones, rats, deadness. What do such repeated images
suggest about the overall message of the poem?

By the waters ... wept echoing Psalm 137: 'By the rivers of Babylon, there
we sat down, yea, we wept'

Leman (a) another name for Lake Geneva; (b) a mistress or prostitute

Mrs Porter a celebrated brothel-keeper

Et O ... coupole (*French*) 'And O those children's voices, singing in the
dome', the final line of 'Parsifal', a sonnet by Paul Verlaine (1844–96),
following Wagner's opera of the same name, about one of the knights in the
Grail legend; choirboys sing at the foot-washing ceremony preceding the
restoration of the Fisher King

Tereu Latin vocative form of Tereus (see note on Philomel at lines
99–100)

Cannon Street Hotel in London, popular with commercial travellers

Metropole hotel in Brighton, weekends at which carry sexual
suggestiveness

Tiresias in Eliot's note, the long passage from Ovid's *Metamorphoses* tells
the legend of Tiresias. He hit two copulating snakes and turned into a
woman; after seven years he did the same thing and turned back into a
man. He was therefore asked to settle a dispute between Jupiter and Juno
as to whether women or men have more pleasure in sex, and said women
do. For this Juno blinded him, but Jupiter gave him the power to know the
future

the sailor home from sea from the penultimate line of 'Requiem', by Robert
Louis Stevenson (1850–94); Eliot's given context is Fragment 149 by
Sappho (sixth century BC): 'Evening Star, who bring home all that bright
Dawn sent out, you bring back sheep, goat and the child to the mother'

Thebes in *Oedipus Tyrannus,* by Sophocles, blind Tiresias 'sees' that the
city has become a waste land because of Oedipus's unwitting incest with
his mother and killing of his father

And walked ... dead in the second book of Homer's *Odyssey,* Tiresias is
consulted by Odysseus in Hades

When lovely ... folly opening of the song referred to by Eliot's note: it is
sung by Olivia, who has been seduced

Weialala ... leiala the Rhine-maidens' lament, in Wagner's opera, *The Twilight of the Gods*, for the theft of the Rhine-gold (another violation that brings a curse)

Highbury ... Richmond and Kew upper-middle-class areas

bore ... Undid me Eliot's Italian quotation from Dante translates 'Remember me, who am La Pia; Siena made me, Maremma unmade me'

Moorgate in the City of London, a lower-middle-class indicator, but also where Eliot worked

Margate Sands seaside resort put in a lower-class context, but also where Eliot recuperated from a nervous breakdown and started *The Waste Land*

IV DEATH BY WATER

Phlebas, the drowned Phoenician sailor

Two weeks after drowning, Phlebas has forgotten his maritime concerns, reduced to bones under the sea – a reminder that death comes to everybody.

Like the other elements in the poem (especially fire that burns in lust but also purifies), water is double-edged: it is needed as life-giving rain to quench the drought of the waste land, but it also takes away life by drowning. The fluid element also underlines the point about fluidity of character and perspective that Eliot makes in his note about Tiresias in line 218: the one-eyed Smyrna merchant, Mr Eugenides (lines 209–14), 'melts into' Phlebas, who also merges with Ferdinand and his supposedly drowned father in *The Tempest* (lines 48, 125, 191, 257). Tracing such links with the rest of the poem – not forgetting the explicit earlier mentions of the drowned Phoenician and the title in lines 47 and 55 – gives a richness of context that the ten lines of this part would not have in isolation, and demonstrates the considerable connectedness of Eliot's 'fragments'.

This fragment can also be fruitfully analysed in itself. What part do the few and irregular **rhymes** play, for instance? By coming and going, rather than being regularly present, do they mirror the theme of the uncertainty and transitoriness of life? Does the to-and-fro **rhythm** likewise mirror the currents that bring about a sea-change

in Phlebas? How does the imagery function? For instance, are the
bones unsettling, upsetting, as in other parts of the poem, especially
when 'Picked', and is 'in whispers' sinister or gently consoling?

title linked to many rituals of death and rebirth, as in Christian baptism or
Jessie Weston's account of an effigy of a fertility god being thrown into the
sea at Alexandria each year and recovered from the Phoenician coast
Phoenician the fourth book of *The Life and Death of Jason* (1867), a poem
by William Morris (1834–96), refers to a drowned Phoenician sailor

V WHAT THE THUNDER SAID

**The voice of the thunder brings a hint of hope to the
dry land**

A time of suffering is marked by the lack of water. One asks another
about a mysterious third person. Civilisation is breaking down. Then
comes 'a damp gust / Bringing rain', and the message of the thunder: be
generous, be compassionate, be self-controlled. There is a memory of
boating, then of fishing, and a series of 'fragments I have shored against
my ruins' before the final blessing of peace.

Part V begins with echoes of Christ's Passion (see notes below),
linked to the first of the three themes Eliot identifies in his notes,
the resurrected Christ's appearance to two disciples on the road to
Emmaus (see Luke 24:13–31), which in turn informs the third
paragraph, which also was 'stimulated', Eliot tells us, by Ernest
Shackleton's account of an Antarctic expedition. These kinds of
interrelatednesses help to unify the sections. Eliot's other two
themes relate more closely to the rest of the whole poem: the 'decay
of eastern Europe' in the fourth and the 'Chapel Perilous', reached
in the final stages of the quest for the Grail, in the fifth paragraph.

Most prominent in this part are the repeated references to water,
which is paradoxically present in the repeated denials of its
presence: 'Here is no water' and 'there is no water', but the word
itself appears eleven times in the second paragraph, together with
mentions of 'drink', 'rain', a 'spring' and a 'pool', and its strongest
sense comes in the lovely lines concluding what Eliot called the

'water-dripping song', where 'the hermit-thrush sings in the pine trees / Drip drop drip drop drop drop drop'. Positive water references recur in the further mentions of actual as well as awaited rain, in the sea episode, and in the fishing on the shore in the last paragraph, where the 'arid plain' is still there but now 'behind' the speaker, who might finally set his lands 'in order' and bring about moral recovery and spiritual peace.

Eliot himself thought Part V 'not only the best part, but the only part that justifies the whole' (letter to Bertrand Russell, 15 October 1923), and it certainly makes a powerful conclusion to the poem, especially in its hints of hope and promise to set against the predominantly bleak and negative vision of each of the earlier parts. Eliot went further in telling Ford Madox Ford, in letters of 14 August and 4 October 1923, that lines 346–58 ('the water-dripping song') were the only *good* lines in the poem: 'The rest is ephemeral'. How do you react to Eliot's opinions? Is 'What the Thunder said' the best part, or do you find any of the others more affecting, or in other ways more effective? Which lines or other aspects of the poem would you single out as not being 'ephemeral'? Clearly, *The Waste Land* has already proved not at all ephemeral. But we still need to decide what it is about it that gives it permanence, that makes it continue to be of value.

For further treatment of *The Waste Land*, see the York Note in this series.

title apart from the Hindu legend to which Eliot's note on line 401 refers, God often speaks in the Bible with a voice of thunder, and thunder often presages rain
the torchlight ... palace a series of echoes of details in Christ's Passion: arrest at night, agony in the garden of Gethsemane, the bringing before the High Priest and then Pilate
lines 366–76 Eliot's German quotation, in his notes, from *Glimpse into Chaos* (1920) by Herman Hesse (1877–1962) translates 'Already half Europe, already at least half of Eastern Europe, on the way to chaos, drives drunkenly in spiritual frenzy along the edge of the abyss and sings as well, sings drunkenly as though singing hymns, as Dmitri Karamazov [in *The*

Brothers Karamazov (1879–80) by Fyodor Dostoevsky (1821–81)] sang. At
these songs the shocked bourgeois laughs; the saint and seer hear them
with tears.'

Ganga the Ganges, India's sacred river

Himavant holy mountain in the Himalayas

I have heard the key ... Eliot's quotation, in his notes, from Dante translates
'and below I heard the door of the horrible tower locked up', spoken by
Count Ugolino, who starves to death in the tower with his sons

Coriolanus the proud title-character of Shakespeare's play is 'broken' by an
appeal from his mother and killed

set my lands in order see Isaiah 38:1: 'Set thine house in order'

Poi ... affina Eliot's full quotation translates '"And so I pray you, by that
virtue which leads you to the top of the stair, be mindful in time of my
pain." Then he hid himself in the fire that refines them.' These words are
from a speech addressed to Dante, as he ascends the third section of the
stairway through Purgatory, by the Provençal poet Arnaut Daniel (*fl.*
*c.*1200), sent there for lustfulness

Quando ... chelidon (*Latin*) 'When shall I be like the swallow?'; the
anonymous poem cited by Eliot, *The Vigil of Venus*, ends with the raped
Philomel turning into a swallow (compare the notes on lines 99–100 above)

Le Prince ... abolie (*French*) 'The Prince of Aquitaine of the ruined tower';
the Spanish title of the sonnet by Gerard de Nerval (1808–55) translates
'The Disinherited', referring to the Prince

THE HOLLOW MEN (1925)

As with *The Waste Land*, this work was built up from a number of
separate poems; the first four sections appeared separately and in different
combinations until the addition of the last section (in *Poems 1909–1925*)
gave us the poem as we now have it.

Though Eliot said he got the title by combining 'The Hollow
Land', a romance by William Morris (1834–96), with 'The Broken Men',
a poem by Rudyard Kipling (1865–1936), it may be more helpful to
remember that Shakespeare gives the phrase 'hollow men' to Brutus
(*Julius Caesar* IV.2.23), as he is pondering the deceitful weakness of his
fellow assassin, Cassius. This would link up with the treachery associated

with the second **epigraph** (see below) and the recollection of another speech by Brutus in Part V of the poem. Further associations with 'hollow' men are provided by the first epigraph (see below). The poem has two epigraphs, on consecutive pages in *Selected Poems*.

'Mistah Kurtz – he dead' is the uneducated announcement of an insolent servant in *Heart of Darkness* (1899), a story by Joseph Conrad (1857–1924) that had a deep effect on Eliot, who thought it an outstanding literary treatment of evil. Set mainly in the darkness of the African jungle, the story explores the darkness at the heart of the so-called civilised men who were sent out there by the European nations during the nineteenth-century 'Scramble for Africa'. Kurtz is such a man, a 'universal genius' who is all the more surely taken over by the darkness, and just before his death is announced he has a vision of this: 'The horror! The horror!' he cries, in words that Eliot planned to use as an epigraph to *The Waste Land*, from discarded bits of which parts of this poem were developed. Even Kurtz, in a story full of hollow men, is described as 'hollow at the core', a 'hollow sham'.

The second epigraph is a version of a chant still used by children begging money for fireworks as they cart about their 'guy', an effigy of Guy Fawkes wearing old clothes and stuffed with straw or paper. This is set alight (as are the fireworks) on the night of Guy Fawkes Day (5 November), the anniversary of the 'Gunpowder Plot' of Roman Catholics to blow up King James and his ministers at the Houses of Parliament on 5 November 1605: on the night before, Guy Fawkes was arrested in the cellar of the House of Lords, guarding nearly two tons of gunpowder.

PART I   **The hopeless state of these empty, passive lives**

The hollow men describe themselves and how the dead remember them (if at all): stuffed like guys, their whispers are 'quiet and meaningless', like their passive and paralysed lives.

> The short lines and the repetitions, varied by **rhymes** and partial rhymes (men … men … when; together … together … cellar; Alas … -less … grass … glass), emphasise the feebleness and limitedness and pointlessness being presented. The verse structure helps to set the tone of the poem as much as the images that will be developed. It is appropriate that the hollow men speak in whispers, and are

remembered by the blessed dead (if at all) as *not* having being
violent, and therefore damned, but just nothing. Eliot thought it
was actually better for humans 'to do evil than to do nothing: at
least, we exist' ('Baudelaire', *Selected Essays*, p. 429). These living
dead are in a kingdom that is 'other' than the capitalised Kingdom
that seems to be the one to which the souls of the blessed pass after
death. The hollow men will in turn join the hopeless band of not
very good, not very bad souls that in Dante (*Hell* III) are not
accepted for Heaven, nor for purging in Purgatory, nor even for
Hell (which wants the decisively bad – the 'lost / Violent souls')
because they have been tepid and indecisive in their lives. While the
damned cross the River Acheron to Hell, these tepid souls are
condemned to stay eternally by the river, in a ghastly Limbo.

dry cellar part of the hopeless and sordid imagery, primarily, but also
setting up possible associations with the cellar where Guy Fawkes kept his
powder dry
Shape without form ... motion four images of things that have lost their
essential meaning, like everything about these people: a shape without form
is shapeless, and so on
Violent souls perhaps such as Guy Fawkes or Kurtz or Caesar's assassins,
decisively 'lost' or damned, unlike the tepidly undecided 'we'

PART II   One of the hollow men speaks

The speaker here shows the timidity of one, afraid of righteous reproach
after death, who wishes to be left with his fragmentary, distant vision – a
scarecrow flapping in the wind.

In this section a personalised 'I' takes up a number of images
used by the 'we' in the first section and develops them. The 'direct
eyes' here cannot be faced even in dreams (sleep imitates death),
and do not appear in the waking nightmare of living death, where
one has only partial glimpses of another life; nor does the 'I' wish
to come nearer those reproachful eyes, as he must do in death. The
'other Kingdom' of Part I is contrasted with this 'dream kingdom'
of living death and the intermediate 'twilight kingdom' where
one's appointed destination (Heaven, Purgatory, Hell, Limbo) is
decided. Other developments include the 'hollow', 'stuffed' dummy

image (in the cellar with rats) that is developed into a scarecrow image (in a field with a dead rat).

Eyes significant in both Dante and *Heart of Darkness*

death's dream kingdom (twice) this kingdom seems to be closest to the 'real' world of the hollow men

There (twice) ambiguous, but seems to refer to the partial vision that sees, not the eyes of the blessed (as in Beatrice's eyes, which Dante at first shame-facedly avoids in *Purgatory*, especially cantos XXX and XXXI), but fragments of that life on the other side of death

Rat's coat, crowskin refers to the farmer's custom of hanging up corpses of pests to frighten off others

crossed staves of a scarecrow, moved about by the wind

twilight kingdom evidently some transitional state (such states are prominent in Eliot: intermediate colours such as violet, intermediate times of day such as twilight and dawn, and so forth) between this life and the next, particularly, perhaps, the time of dying itself

PART III   The 'dead land' of the hollow men

A presentation of the desert waste, where useless stone idols receive the attention of the loveless.

There is further development of the images of decay and meaninglessness from the 'broken glass' (which has lost its usefulness) in Part I, through the 'broken column' glimpsed in Part II, to the 'broken stone' here of useless stone images: the man who prays to such an idol is already doomed to death. For the first time, a hint of suppressed sexual love is clearly given ('Waking alone ... kiss'), throwing further light on the dried-up condition of the hollow men.

stone images ... broken stone as in 'your images shall be broken ... your idols may be broken', Ezekiel 6:4,6

death's other kingdom it is hard to know whether the lower-case 'k' is intended to distinguish this other kingdom of death from that in Part I; perhaps this kingdom is where all the damned dead go

Lips that would kiss / Form prayers evidently as a second-best activity, as in a line by James Thomson (1834–82) from his poem 'Art', 'Lips only sing when they cannot kiss'; there is also Juliet's 'lips that they [the holy] must use in prayer [not kissing]' (*Romeo and Juliet*, I.5.101)

PART IV The end of these lost lives, for whom there is no blessed vision

For the hollow men there are no eyes (of the blessed dead again?) to be found in their 'hollow valley' with its dying stars, nor, as they gather by the river, the star or rose that could give hope to them.

The culmination of the eyes and star and death and hollow men imagery is found here, with the clearest indications of both the damned waiting, silent and sightless, by the river of Hell and the blessed with their star and rose.

broken jaw image of desolation and lack of ability to communicate; and a possible contrast with the unbroken 'jawbone of an ass' with which Samson slew a thousand Philistines (Judges 15:15)

our lost kingdoms not of death this time, but of men, and their illusions

tumid river corresponds with Dante's presentation (*Hell* III) of the River Acheron that flows round Hell: on the bank ('beach'), their last meeting place, the souls of the dead wait to be ferried across

the perpetual star a contrast with the 'fading' and 'dying' stars earlier in the poem, this description recalls both the 'living star' of Dante's vision of the Virgin Mary (*Heaven* XXIII, 92) and the 'single star' (XXXI, 28) of the Light of God

Multifoliate rose recalls Dante's vision of the highest Heaven as a rose, with the Virgin and other saints forming the many petals (*foglia* is 'petal' in Italian) in *Heaven* XXX and the following cantos, but Mary herself is described as a rose in Canto XXIII, 73 – just before she is called a 'living star' (see previous note)

death's twilight kingdom a transitional region (see note on 'twilight kingdom' in Part II above) where (only) the hollow men have still the (vain) hope of seeing the beatific vision

only perhaps deliberately ambiguous, this could mean the vision is only the hope (not the actual fate) of the empty men or/and only such men would have such a hope; it would be hard to make it mean the blessed vision is their 'only hope', especially as all they can expect (hope for) is a hopeless existence as in Dante's Limbo

PART V   The final desperate vision

An adapted children's round mimics the meaningless round of unfulfilled lives, followed by a meditation – interrupted by broken speaking of life and the highest Kingdom – on the 'Shadow', which is whatever in men's lives, after something is proposed, prevents its realisation, coming between what might be and what actually is: between idea and reality, a desire and its fulfilment, and so on. Another chant presents the pathetic end of this world.

In this final section the most notable feature is one of tone change, both in the change from the previous sections and the changes within the conclusion itself. The critic F.R. Leavis (1895–1978) finely observed here the 'nightmare poise over the grotesque' (*New Bearings in English Poetry*, Penguin, 1963, p. 96), which applies to the whole balancing act that can move from the bizarre opening chant to the sombre truth of the intervening Shadow, and on through the meditative fragments to the final chant's 'whimper'. The last Kingdom is the highest, the Kingdom of God: the poet, barely able to approach even the thought of it, stammers out broken phrases. The broken lives presented throughout the poem fade away in a conclusion combining a feeble trailing off with a memorable inevitability.

It is Eliot's bleakest poetic vision, a vision of dry lives lacking the clear element of hope (the promise of rain) which even 'Gerontion' and *The Waste Land* have. From now on, however, the way can only be upwards.

Here we go round ... morning a parody of a children's chant, imitating 'Here we go round the mulberry bush' and 'Here we go gathering nuts in May', both originating in fertility dances

prickly pear this cactus, flourishing in desert soil, gives a pointed twist to the expected fertility **symbol**

five o'clock the traditional hour of Christ's resurrection; dawn dances are common in Mayday and other rituals of the cycles of renewal after death

motion ... act recalls other words of Brutus (*Julius Caesar* II.1.63–5): 'Between the acting of a dreadful thing / And the first motion, all the interim is / Like a phantasma, or a hideous dream'

The hollow men: V continued

Falls the Shadow Eliot agreed that he derived this phrase from the best-known poem by Ernest Dowson (1867–1900), 'Non sum qualis eram bonae sub regno Cynarae' (Horace: 'I am not as I was beneath the reign of good Cynara'), in which we find 'There fell thy shadow' and 'Then falls thy shadow'. Other relevant associations of shadow may be found in many places elsewhere, from the tormenting shadows of *Heart of Darkness* back to 'the valley of the shadow of death' in Psalm 23

For Thine is the Kingdom from the Lord's Prayer ('Our Father')

Life is very long this phrase appears in Conrad's novel *The Outcast of the Islands* (1896), where a broken man is to be punished by being kept alive rather than killed; it reads in the poem as an exhausted reversal of the usual idea that life is short but art is long. For 'conception' and 'creation', 'emotion' and 'response' apply as much to art as to life; indeed, at one level the poem is a commentary on artistic as well as spiritual and sexual sterility

essence ... descent according to the Greek philosopher Plato (*c*.428–*c*.348BC), the essence or ideal, spiritual form descends to a lower material reality to take physical form

This is the way ... the parodied children's song returns, as in 'This is the way we (clap our hands)'

Not with a bang as hoped for by Guy Fawkes, or those with visions of a grand violence at earth's end, or those who idiomatically wish to go out (from life, a job, etcetera) 'with a bang', that is, impressively; the phrase also recalls the account by George Santayana (1863–1952), who taught Eliot at Harvard, of the *Divine Comedy* ending 'not with a bang, with some casual incident, but in sustained reflection'

whimper this feeble sound contrasts appropriately with a bang. In Rudyard Kipling's poem 'Danny Deever', the soul of a soldier executed for cowardice 'whimpers' overhead as it passes; Eliot thought Kipling's choice of 'whimpers' was 'exactly right'

Ash-Wednesday (1930)

This and the remaining poems in *Selected Poems* were all published after Eliot's reception into the Church of England as a convert (Latin *convertere*, to turn about). The title refers to the first day of Lent, the forty days of fasting (as Christ fasted in the wilderness) and turning from sin towards godliness that precede the Easter celebration of Christ's resurrection. The poem is full of references to the liturgy of this day, named after the traditional ash cross marked by the priest on the foreheads of the congregation. For instance, the poem takes up the reading for the Epistle that begins at Joel 2:12: 'Turn ye even to me, saith the Lord'.

PART I   A statement of renunciation by the convert

The convert renounces everything in his past in order to learn the passive way to God: getting away from ephemeral things like ambition, glory and power, even from nature and love, he prays to escape himself and his self-consciousness, and to achieve serenity and religious peace.

The simple words and repetitions immediately effect an impression of the 'small and dry' voice of a man struggling to make clear what is complex, as in the simple language used to utter deep thoughts in Dante, in the Bible, and in Roman Catholic and Anglican liturgy, the three underlying sources of the entire poem. It seems the 'I' of the poem is not the dramatised consciousness of a created character, as in previous poems, but the poet speaking directly in his own person, and his concerns are no longer aesthetic and worldly but spiritual and other-worldly.

Because I do not hope to turn again a translation of 'Perch 'io non spero di tornar giammai', the opening line of a poem by the Italian Guido Cavalcanti (1255–1300) lamenting his exile and expecting never to see his lady again. When Part I was first published, as a separate poem, it was entitled 'Perch 'io Non Spero'

Desiring … scope a version ('gift' instead of 'art') of a line from Shakespeare's Sonnet 29, where the poet's discontent with his lot turns to joy when he thinks of his beloved. A renunciation of poetry seems to be implied in this section – or at least of the former type of poetry

agèd eagle reputed to be able to renew its youth and vigour (as in Psalm 103)

infirm glory a phrase used in *Night and Day* (1919), a novel by Virginia Woolf (1882–1941), to refer to the once famous, now old

time ... place implied contrasts with eternity and infinity

blessèd face in rejecting even this (which recalls especially the face of Dante's Beatrice), the convert rejects both an earlier love and a beatific vision as a way of turning to God

the voice including his own former poetic voice?

vans not only an archaic word for 'wings', this also means the 'fans' which are used in winnowing chaff from grain

to care about godly things

not to care about worldly things that need to be renounced

to sit still the passive way for the soul to prepare for God, as described by the Spanish mystic, St John of the Cross (1542–91); in his *Pensées*, the French philosopher and physicist Blaise Pascal (1623–62) thinks 'all the troubles of man come from his not knowing how to sit still'

Pray for us ... death conclusion of a prayer to the Virgin Mary, asking her to plead with God for sinners

PART II   The convert rejoices in his dry bones

Addressing the Lady, the convert describes how he has become dead to his former life, and how his bones are glad he has 'forgotten' his deeds, even his love, through the Lady who is – among other paradoxes – the Rose of forgetfulness as well as memory, and are glad to be scattered.

When first published separately, Part II was entitled 'Salutation'. This underlines the links with both Beatrice (who salutes Dante in *The New Life*, III, dressed in pure white) and the Virgin (saluted by the Angel Gabriel as well as the devout): as in Dante, a parallel between these two Ladies is established in the poem, and they are basic to its total imagery. But the imagery is not necessarily limited by such specific references: the Rose also recalls the whole courtly love tradition implied by the medieval *Romance of the Rose*, the Garden also recalls the Garden of Eden, and so forth. The first and third verse-paragraphs of this section use imagery of bones and the desert, and contrast this with trees and coolness, associated with the capitalised Garden of the second paragraph, and all three paragraphs play on variations of the verb 'forget'. By such means a feeling of comparative looseness in superficial form is given a tighter underlying framework.

Lady recalls Beatrice, agent of Dante's salvation, and devoted attendant on the Virgin Mary in Paradise

white colour of purity used for three descriptions in this section: leopards, Lady, bones

leopards here seeming to destroy on God's orders, as in the Bible (for example, Jeremiah 5:6)

juniper-tree this **symbol** of cleansing and rebirth appears in 'The Juniper-Tree', a fairy tale retold by the German Brothers Grimm, Jacob (1785–1863) and Wilhelm (1786–1859), in which a murdered child's bones, put beneath a juniper, are miraculously restored to life; another miracle appears in the biblical story of Elijah, who prayed for death under a juniper in the wilderness and was sent food by God instead (1 Kings 19:1–8)

my legs ... skull organs representing activity, emotion, sensuality and thought

Shall these bones live in the vision of Ezekiel in the valley of dry bones, God asks 'can these bones live?' before restoring them to life (Ezekiel 37:3)

dissembled a pun on disguised and dis-assembled

Prophesy to the wind the words of God in Ezekiel 37:9, to put breath back into the bodies made from the restored bones

bones sang appears twice, as does 'chirping', to stress the happiness, as in Psalm 51 (often sung on Ash-Wednesday in addition to the 'Proper' Psalms): 'Make me to hear joy and gladness; that the bones which thou hast broken may rejoice'

burden (a) plague; (b) tune: a punning allusion to 'the grasshopper shall be a burden' (Ecclesiastes 12:5)

Lady of silences ... all love ends an imitation of the Litany of the Blessed Virgin Mary, where she is addressed as 'Rose', 'Mother', and so on; Eliot's idea of the combination of opposites ('Calm and distressed' etcetera) is presumably developed from her essential paradox as Virgin and Mother

in the cool of the day description of God's walk in the Garden of Eden (Genesis 3:8)

This is the land ... lot God's words in Ezekiel 48:29

PART III   The convert's history

The turnings of the convert's spiritual progress are here imaged in the climbing of a staircase, as he turns away from the attractive as well as the unattractive aspects of his former life in the world.

At its first, separate publication, Part III was entitled 'Som de
L'Escalina' ('The top of the staircase'); for the full context of the
Italian words, see the notes above on 'Poi ... affina' in Part V of *The
Waste Land.* This section develops both the staircase image and the
idea that sensual distractions hinder spiritual progress. These
memories, lovingly recalled, contrast vividly with the 'old man' and
'agèd shark' of the spiritual struggle.

same shape as himself, in an earlier struggle
devil ... despair Eliot thought the 'demon of doubt' was 'inseparable from
the spirit of belief'
fig's fruit begins a series of distracting recollections of the sensuous world
figure ... flute a medievalised pagan figure, perhaps to be associated with
Pan, the amorous and pipe-playing god of pastoral life in Greek mythology
Lilac as the context shows, the flower is associated with a memory of past
love
Lord, I am not worthy ... only the words of humility spoken in the Mass, from
Matthew 8:8: 'Lord, I am not worthy that thou shouldst come under my
roof: but speak the word only and my servant shall be healed' (in liturgical
use, 'soul' can be substituted for 'servant')

PART IV   The silent sister's holy message

In the peace of the garden, a nun-like figure walks about and wordlessly
signals a message of redemption.

The chief problem of interpretation has always been the
relationship of the veiled sister and the Lady of Part II: all we
can say, looking ahead to the rest of the poem, is that both are
associated with Mary and Beatrice; more specific identification
is probably restricting, though tempting. For it may be that the
very obscurity and impersonality of this section reveal a too
personal association that Eliot is covering up, as he did when
removing the original dedication of the poem, 'To My Wife'. Some
readers, for instance, see a reference to Vivienne's hospitalisation,
the 'sister' being a nursing sister, a role often taken by nuns. But
there are only hints, and perhaps the reader should concentrate on
the public 'meaning' of the poem throughout.

violet (a) the colour is associated with both transition (as at dawn and dusk) and repentance; (b) the flower is associated with both resurrection and purity

Mary's colour blue; but sometimes also white

trivial may include a pun on the origin of this word: where *three roads* meet, the basic experiences of learning and life (see the three dreams in Part VI)

ignorance ... knowledge not knowing such suffering in herself, perhaps, yet knowing of the suffering of others

larkspur blue flower (delphinium)

Sovegna vos 'Be mindful', the plea of Arnaut Daniel (*Purgatory* XXVI, 147) that the punishment for lust should be kept in mind by Dante (see Part III above and Part V of *The Waste Land*)

Redeem / The time by, as St Paul advised in his Epistles, using one's time wisely

the higher dream in his 'Dante' essay, Eliot associates the Divine Pageant in *Purgatory* XXIX, in which Beatrice's chariot is drawn by a griffon, with 'the world of what I call the *high dream,* and the modern world seems capable only of the *low dream*'. The hearse in the next line seems to mourn the passing of the higher dream

veiled as are nuns, followers of Mary, and Beatrice; also mourners

yews trees associated with churchyards, and hence death, but also with immortality, because evergreen and long-lived

garden god ... flute suggests Pan once more (see Part III)

And after this our exile from the *Salve Regina* ('Hail, Queen'), a prayer to the Virgin continuing 'show unto us the blessed fruit of thy womb, Jesus'

PART V   A lamentation for the unconverted

In a chanting litany of lamentation, with much echoing wordplay, distressed regret is expressed for those who do not hear and surrender to the Word of God. The speaker wonders if the veiled sister will pray for these unconverted, unregenerate sinners who walk in darkness, and cries out in reproachful anguish to them.

The word-play in Part V is often criticised as excessive, not so much in the opening Andrewes-style turning round and round of particular phrases to be examined as in the elaborate internal

rhymes ('found ... Resound', 'mainland ... rainland', etcetera) of the central passages.

The Word without a word part of a development based on the opening of St John's Gospel and the Christmas 1618 sermon of Lancelot Andrewes: see notes on the similar usage in 'Gerontion'

And the light ... as in John 1:5

unstilled because ever-turning, as well as ever-disobedient to the Word

world ... whirled a pun found in *Orchestra*, a poem by John Davies (1565–1618): 'Behold the world, how it is whirled round!'

O my people ... thee from Micah 6:3, used in Christ's Reproaches from the Cross in the Good Friday liturgy

affirm the faith

deny the old life

desert in the garden the death of the old life of sensuous delights but spiritual emptiness

garden in the desert the spiritual rebirth brought about by desolation and suffering

PART VI   **The convert elaborates his first statement, and again prays for serenity**

The convert acknowledges the pull of his past life, and especially love, but prays for help to find peace with God.

The opening 'Although' takes us back to the 'Because' of Part I and adds its qualification: although he hopes his conversion is final, the convert clearly recognises the pull of old desires, movingly presented in the memories of the sea and the love he has lost. As the time of conversion (the dying of the old man and the birth of the new) is difficult, the help of the blessed teachers is needed. Here the poet brings together all the previous female presences in the poem to aid his final prayer.

Much may have been unclear or laboured, much may have seemed to depend on biblical, liturgical and Dante-esque catch phrases that can do the poet's work for him, much may have been hard to swallow for those who do not share Eliot's renunciatory attitude – but as an enacted vision of the convert, with its cumulative power of imagery and incantation, *Ash-Wednesday* can also be deeply moving.

dreamcrossed twilight ... dying as in the 'twilight kingdom' in *The Hollow Men*

Bless me father [for I have sinned] opening words of the penitent to the priest at Confession

lost lilac once again a memory of lost love

ivory gates through which false dreams pass from the underworld to earth; such delusions are created by the eye that is blind to the true Word

three dreams perhaps three such hopes of fulfilment as the artistic, the sexual and the spiritual; perhaps three such states of desire as consciousness, memory and dream, etcetera

sit still see note on this phrase in Part I

Our peace in His will the words of the nun Piccarda (see 'A Cooking Egg') in *Paradiso* III, 85

Suffer me ... separated [from Thee] from the ancient hymn *Anima Christi* ('Soul of Christ')

And let my cry ... Thee liturgical response to the priest's words, 'Hear my prayer, O Lord' (from Psalm 102)

ARIEL POEMS

The four poems in this section were published by Faber and Faber in successive years as a kind of Christmas card. The first three have clear Christmas associations, with the first two relating specifically to the birth of Christ, and the rather different Shakespearian fourth records another miraculous event.

JOURNEY OF THE MAGI (1927)

A recollection of the Magi's journey

One of the Magi recalls their hard journey: the cold of midwinter and other difficulties along the route, coming to a temperate valley, and finally reaching their destination. Unexpectedly, he describes not the joyful but the saddening and hard-to-bear results of having witnessed the holy Birth.

As in 'Gerontion', this is the **monologue** of an old man reviewing the past; as in *Ash-Wednesday*, he and his companions have to struggle against the old life: not only when the tough journey made them long for summer, silken girls, sherbet (a refreshing drink); not only the difficult acceptance of the Word; but even the suffering caused by alienation from their own people, still holding to their heathen gods. The journey is not over yet.

The imagery of the middle section is particularly unusual, both for the prophetic suggestions of future events of the Crucifixion (a literary technique called **prolepsis**) and for the significance of the choice of the other images. Of such apparently random but emotion-charged images Eliot has written illuminatingly in *The Use of Poetry and the Use of Criticism* (Faber and Faber, 1964, p. 148):

six ruffians seen through an open window playing cards at night at a small French railway junction where there was a watermill: such memories may have symbolic value, but of what we cannot tell, for they come to represent the depths of feeling into which we cannot peer.

Magi the three wise men who came from the East with gifts for the newly born Jesus. See Matthew 2:1–12

'A cold ... of winter' the quoted words are adapted from the 1622 Christmas Day sermon by Bishop Andrewes: 'A cold coming they had of it at this time of the year, just the worst time of the year to take a journey, and specially a long journey in. The ways deep, the weather sharp ... "the very dead of winter"'

three trees there were to be three crosses at the Crucifixion for Christ and the two thieves

white horse in Revelation 19:11, Christ rides a white horse in glory

dicing ... silver the Roman soldiers diced for the clothes of the crucified Christ, who was betrayed for thirty pieces of silver

set down / This a phrase used by Andrewes in the same sermon (and elsewhere); here the old Magus is addressing his implied listener(s), anxious that no aspect of his story should be missed

Birth or Death because one must 'die' to the old life before being 'born' to the new life in Christ: see *Ash-Wednesday*

these Kingdoms traditionally the Magi were also kings

the old dispensation that is, pre-Christ
another death into eternal life this time (as promised by Christ)?

A SONG FOR SIMEON (1928)

A development of the biblical Song of Simeon

Simeon, old and waiting to die, prays to God and looks forward to the times of trouble after his death, but he has (as promised) seen the Infant Jesus, and is satisfied.

This is another **monologue** of a tired old man, waiting for death, but he is much more peaceful and accepting than Gerontion, and the movement of the verse is even more simple and gentle than that of the old Magus in the previous poem. This effect is assisted by repeating **rhymes** more than once: 'and', 'stand', 'hand', 'land' and so on. However, the simplicity does not preclude the possibility of sophisticated metrics, notably in the placing of the biblical extracts, and complex imagery, notably in the opening verse paragraph.

Simeon in the Bible story this 'just and devout' Jew, promised by the Holy Ghost that he shall not die before he has seen Christ, takes the baby in his arms in the temple and can die happy. His Song is sung at Evening Prayer (*Nunc dimittis*): 'Lord, now lettest thou thy servant depart in peace, according to thy word: for mine eyes have seen thy salvation, which thou hast prepared before the face of all people; a light to lighten the Gentiles, and the glory of thy people Israel'; see Luke 2:29–32. The poem repeats phrases from this canticle, and develops other ideas in Simeon's story
Lord as in the Bible Song, Simeon's first word
Roman Judaea was then under Roman rule
hyacinths spring flowers of death and rebirth, but here artificially grown indoors in the winter: an image of Simeon's amazing 'spring' in the winter of his old age
Grant ... peace a liturgical echo of Simeon's prayer
time of sorrow Simeon begins looking ahead to the persecution of the Christians: in Luke 2:34–5, he prophesies the suffering to come
cords and scourges as used when Christ was whipped by the Romans
stations hints at the Stations of the Cross (events of the Crucifixion)

mountain of desolation the hill of Calvary, but, as in all these images, capable of extension to the later sufferings of Christ's followers

maternal sorrow Mary witnessed the Crucifixion

birth season of decease a typical play on the idea of dying into life, especially appropriate to this very old man

Infant ... Word more verbal play derived from the *Verbum Infans* sermon (1618) of Andrewes: see notes to 'Gerontion'

saints' stair see *Ash-Wednesday* III

Not for me ... he will not himself experience the suffering and the ecstatic vision of the Christian saints and martyrs

(And a sword ... also) in Luke 2:35, Simeon warns Mary in just such a parenthesis: '(Yea, a sword shall pierce through thy own soul also)'; once more, of course, Eliot's usage is capable of extension, even to the reader

ANIMULA (1929)

The progress of a 'little soul'

The development of the simple soul is traced from the explorations of childhood, beginning with the physical and continuing through the moral and mental and spiritual, to the paralysis grown from experience; the poem ends with a prayer.

Some readers find the **rhythms**, if not the **rhymes**, rather monotonous, and the poem generally lacking in poetic (as opposed to philosophic) energy and inventiveness. But the child's eye view of the world is sensitively recreated, and the different last section can come to seem, with familiarity, more suggestive than mystifying.

Animula a little soul, as in the first line of a poem addressed to his soul by the Emperor Hadrian (AD76–138): 'Animula vagula blandula' ('Little soul, wandering, pleasing')

'Issues ... soul' this quotation derives from a passage in Dante's *Purgatory* discussing the nature of the soul and its need of control; Eliot gives the following translation in his 'Dante' essay of Canto XVI, lines 85 to 96: 'From the hands of Him who loves her before she is, there issues like a little child that plays, with weeping and laughter, the simple soul, that knows nothing except that, come from the hands of a glad creator, she turns willingly to everything that delights her. First she tastes the flavour of a trifling good;

then is beguiled, and pursues it, if neither guide nor check withhold her. Therefore laws were needed as a curb; a ruler was needed, who should at least see afar the tower of the true City'

running stags may include a reference to the legendary Actaeon, the hunter turned into a stag and killed by his own hounds (see also the second last line of the poem)

imperatives moral considerations that impel us to action

'is and seems' as in *Appearance and Reality* (1893), by the philosopher F.H. Bradley (1846–1924), on whom Eliot completed a Harvard thesis in 1916: the difference between appearance ('seems') and reality ('is')

Encyclopaedia Britannica the largest and best-known encyclopaedia in English

Issues ... time ... this variation of the first line begins the stage where experience (time) has distorted the soul

Denying ... blood rejecting the impulsive demands of feeling

viaticum (a) communion given to the dying, from (b) what is provided for the soul's sustenance on its journey

Guiterriez Eliot intended this to represent (especially by **onomatopoeia**?) the 'successful person of the machine age'

Boudin similarly intended to represent (from the French slang sense, 'explosive', of a word used normally for a blood pudding, which has the shape of a sausage – 'banger' in English slang) someone who was blown up in the First World War

Floret Eliot said this figure was 'entirely imaginary', but perhaps suggestive of 'folklore memories'. He is reminiscent of the legendary Actaeon (see note on 'running stags' above) and the god Attis in ancient fertility myths, killed by a wild boar, as was Adonis, who turned into a flower (Latin *floret*, he flowers): the connection with the cycle of death and rebirth seems clear, at any rate

Pray ... birth the change from the expected concluding 'death' in this prayer (see *Ash-Wednesday* I) points to both the soul's birth into the new life and the need for prayer at the other beginning of the soul's journey, ordinary birth, before the child's life is corrupted in the ways the poem has shown

MARINA (1930)

A father meditates in wonderment on his daughter

Beautiful images from nature are recollected by the father as he considers the return of his daughter, and the harsh natural images associated with sin evaporate in the same beauty. Gazing wonderingly at his child, and associating her and himself with the boat he made, he is prepared to give up his life for hers, as he lovingly returns to the opening images and her restored presence.

This, the most touching and emotional of all the *Selected Poems*, uses the most powerfully affecting natural images, fluctuating rhythms, and rhyming echoes that come and go, to parallel the to-and-fro, wondering feelings of the father who is the speaker. Highly moving in style as much as in subject, its tenderness is reflected in the delicacies of its poetic movement, where all that is harsh is 'dissolved' and loving wonderment takes over. It is the most positive and life-affirming of all Eliot's works.

For further discussion, see Text 3 of Extended Commentaries.

title the daughter of Pericles, in Shakespeare's *Pericles*. She is associated with the sea because she was born at sea (*Marina* is the Latin feminine adjective for 'marine', 'of the sea'): sea imagery is appropriately central to the poem also. In the play, the grown Marina, believed by her father to be long dead, is restored to him in what seems to him a miracle: this 'recognition' scene (V.1) Eliot considered one of the finest moments in literature

epigraph the words of Hercules as he comes out of the madness in which he killed his wife and children ('What place is this, what region, what part of the world?') in the tragedy *Hercules Furens* (line 1138) by Seneca (*c*.4BC–AD65)

Those who sharpen ... a series of 'Death' images follows: those who use weapons; the vain; the complacent; the sexual

hummingbird the change from the manuscript's more usual 'peacock' probably reflects Eliot's recollection of *The Boy Hunters* (1853), an adventure story by Mayne Reid (1818–83) in which a hummingbird's throat 'glitters' (p. 110)

Given or lent echoes 'Given, not lent', a line by Alice Meynell (1847–1922) in her poem 'Unto Us a Son is Given', referring to Christ (the biblical prophecy of Isaiah 9:6)

stars ... eye an image of transcendence ('beyond-ness') coexisting with an image of immanence ('within-ness')

Whispers ... leaves the image of hidden children recurs in Eliot; he derived it from Kipling's story 'They', in which ghostly children frolic about a blind woman's house and the narrator's own dead daughter powerfully reappears

I made this ... this section points to the relationships between himself and vessel, vessel and daughter, himself and daughter; both his creations are contrasts, yet both are 'vessels' of redemption

garboard strake first range of planks next to the keel in the bottom of a boat

CHORUSES FROM 'THE ROCK' (1934)

The Rock, a pageant-play, was written for a church fund-raising campaign in London. Eliot provided some of the prose dialogue in this largely unimpressive work, but the verse choruses were his major contribution, and the only parts that he thought worth preserving. For *Selected Poems* he chose six of the ten choruses.

The pageant is about the building of a church, and particularly about the difficulties of building the Invisible Church in the modern world.

CHORUS I   **The need of the modern world for the Church**

The Chorus notes the ways in which life's unending, futile circlings have led to the modern world being further than ever from God, and the Church unwanted. 'The Rock' (St Peter) dispenses religious advice and points out the permanent opposition of Good and Evil, the modern ignoring of the spiritual wasteland or desert, and the good in building. The workmen then chant about building a Church together, are responded to by the complaints of the unemployed, and chant again about the need for building and having a job for everyone.

The Chorus itself, as in classical Greek drama, is primarily there to provide a commentary on the action, and speaks in the first person.

The biblical language, with many images and phrases and cadences drawn from the Bible (some of which are noted below), is fundamental to the whole of *The Rock*, but it is mixed with ordinary colloquial speech to give an up-to-date yet timeless feel to the verse: for instance, in the 'desert' chant, the modern 'tube-train' sits next to the eternal 'heart of your brother'. As you read through this and the following Choruses, look out for changes in the verse when the Chorus changes emotional direction, as from pleading to anger, or meditative calm to ecstatic joy.

Eagle ... Hunter these constellations are here used mainly to introduce the endless cycles of creation, hence the choice of ones whose names stress movement ('soars', 'pursues')

the Word of God

twenty centuries since Christ

Dust as God told Adam, 'dust thou art, and unto dust shalt thou return' (Genesis 3:19)

timekept City financial area of London, ruled by the need for timekeeping (London has many church clocks with bells), as are its office workers

foreign flotations pun on (a) overseas ships and (b) loans for overseas businesses (London was then the centre of world trade)

chop-houses restaurants with cheap, ready-prepared food (useful for hurried businessmen)

six days, on the seventh part of a parody of the religious observance of the Sabbath (from God's rest on the seventh day of creation: Genesis 22–3)

Hindhead ... Maidenhead beauty spots near London

The Rock he is revealed at the end as Saint Peter (Christ's 'this rock': see 'The Hippopotamus'), but represents in a more general way those disciples who suffer for faith, bear witness to the Word, criticise the worldly, and so on. The whole 'rock' image relates also to God as a support, a frequent biblical usage, as in 2 Samuel 22:2: 'The Lord is my rock'

I have trodden the winepress alone from Isaiah 63:3: the biblical **metaphor** of treading on grapes (to make juice for wine) is used for those who follow the orders (often angry) of God

Make perfect your will to serve God, a biblical instruction Eliot may have come to via Dante's *Heaven* XXXIII, 103–5

take no thought as in Matthew 6:34: 'Take therefore no thought for the morrow'

Good and Evil for Eliot a clearcut and vital distinction; but compare Chorus X

the Unemployed of whom there were millions in the Depression of the 1930s

No man has hired us the words of the unemployed labourers in Matthew 20:7

In this land ... begins a parody of God's promise of a prosperous land for the faithful, as in Jeremiah 32:41, 43

shortened bed ... narrow sheet adapted from Isaiah 28:20

CHORUS II   The need for the Church to be always building

This Chorus argues that church-building is futile without the spiritual dimension, and leaves a useless ruin, much as empire-building leaves uncertainty back home. The Church needs to go through a perpetual cycle of decay and renewal and, in response to the legacy (for good and ill) of our ancestors and in the face of the modern lack of interest in a sense of community, has much to do, urgently.

The long sentences in this Chorus are closer to prose than poetry: the feeling is that we are listening to the exhortations of a sermon. Think what it is about the language that strikes you as more prosaic or more poetic.

There is also a notable to-and-fro movement between different tenses. For example, the past of history in the opening phrase, 'Thus your fathers were', is contrasted with the present situation of 'you now sit helpless' by the end of the sentence; the past-tense paragraph beginning 'When your fathers fixed', introducing the fuller history lesson about imperial expansion, precedes the present-tense paragraph about inheritance, with 'you eat the fruit' and the rest, which includes future indications in the imperative mood ('the Church must'), also found in the final imperatives ('Let the work ... Let the clay ... let the saw ... Let the fire ...'). These shifts mirror the sense of the Church being forever built in the past, and decaying in the present, and needing rebuilding in the future.

Christ ... cornerstone traditional development of Psalm 118: 'The stone which the builders refused has become the head stone of the corner'

Spirit ... waters as in Genesis 1:2, at the Creation

tortoise perhaps a reference to a Hindu creation myth in which the world is on the tortoise's back

love our neighbour a central requirement of Christians, as in Matthew 19:19 (citing Leviticus 19:18): 'love thy neighbour as thyself'

citizenship ... Heaven as in 'fellow-citizens with the saints, and of the household of God' (Ephesians 2:19)

Whipsnade a zoo near London

imperial expansion an account of the British Empire follows

prosperity ... adversity opposites used, for example, in the Book of Common Prayer ('both in prosperity and adversity')

ribbon roads with 'ribbons' of houses on either side, as in London in the 1920s and 1930s

CHORUS III   A denunciation of Godless modern lives

The opening denounces the modern generation of the so-called 'enlightened' who are nevertheless benighted in their secular futilities. Two voices prophesy dereliction in irreligious London, then the Chorus returns to the notion of building being futile without God, with another list of Godless modern enterprises seen as vain and empty.

This Chorus is an imitation of the way the prophets in the Bible bring 'the Word of the Lord' to an erring people, and is appropriately full of biblical echoes. Particularly striking are the emphatic questions – most emphatic in the second and fourth verse-paragraphs, when they are shorter and closer on each other's heels – and the emphatic repetitions throughout. The latter are most readily seen by looking at how many lines have recurring opening words: 'O ... O', 'I have given you' opening six consecutive lines, 'Many ... Many ... Many', 'Much ... Much', 'I have loved ... I have swept', 'Or ... Or', 'To ... To ... To', and 'Engaged in' opening three consecutive lines, to underline the vacuity of such activities. Closer inspection will reveal other repetitions operating partly *within* lines, as with 'In the land ... The rabbit ... the thorn ... The nettle ... the gravel court ... the wind',

or the participles in the sequence 'Binding ... Exploiting ...
developing ... Dividing ... devising ... working ... printing ...
Plotting ... flinging ... Turning'. These plentiful incantatory
repetitions add to the questions in giving urgency as well as
emphasis to the poetic and prophetic utterance of this whole
Chorus. Can you think of other ways in which these or other
devices operate in these Choruses?

designing (a) planning; (b) crafty

enlightened as in the Age of Reason, or Enlightenment, rational thought
may bring rejection of the spiritual

East the East End of London, with its dockland slums

goat part of a prophecy, not a description

North ... West ... South the wealthier middle-class areas outside London,
later in the poem characterised by their gardens, tennis and golf

build in vain ... keep the City as in the opening of Psalm 127: 'Except the
Lord build the house, they labour in vain that build it: except the Lord keep
the city, the watchman waketh but in vain'

I have loved ... echoes Psalm 26: 'Lord, I have loved the habitation of thy
house'

House of God (traditional way of referring to temple or church)

the Stranger one of the titles of 'The Rock' in the first Chorus; later
associated with Death

common and preferred the stars anciently indicate men's fortune; modern
men seek another fortune on the stock exchange in ordinary or preference
shares

CHORUS VII   **From God at the beginning to the present gods**

This Chorus traces religious history from the creation of the world and
the earliest struggles towards God, through the establishment of the
'Higher Religions', to Christ as the one way. But now men have no god,
or rather, the present gods are entirely secular: after Reason first displaced
God, the objects of worship have become things like Money and Power,
faith has become belief in things like Life, Race or Marxism. After the
unemployed from the first Chorus are heard again, mankind's disregard
of the Church is linked to the only gods now flourishing: the cuttingly
unspiritual 'Usury, Lust and Power'.

A vast stretch of history is here compressed into four paragraphs before the fragments of speech of the unemployed and the final questions and comments of the Chorus. The first paragraph deals with the Creation, with appropriate quotations from Genesis; the next presents the 'Higher Religions', which led men to the light but came to 'a dead end'; then there is Christ, the one accepted way to come to the light; and the fourth paragraph lambasts the atheism of the present age, which 'advances progressively backwards'. In the first three paragraphs there is the repeated assertion of light leading to light, but 'light' is significantly absent from the modern age, which has only the 'darkness on the face of the deep'. This biblical quotation appears, joined with the repetition of another phrase with a biblical echo, 'Waste and void', in each section except the one devoted to Christ, to underline the difference between the truly enlightened Christian way and both the earlier strivings towards the light and the benighted state of the present that the Chorus bewails.

The four paragraphs could be described as prose poetry or poetic prose. Rather as with Chorus II, where do you think the emphasis should lie: more on prose or more on poetry? What part do the repetitive and biblical phrasings play in shaping your response?

In the beginning … void … deep from the account of Creation in Genesis 1:1–2

Higher Religions as of the Jews and Muslims

knowledge of Good and Evil a development into something good (for Eliot, as in Chorus I: but see also Chorus X) of the forbidden 'tree of the knowledge of good and evil' in Genesis 2:17

Prayer wheels used especially by Tibetan Buddhists

worship of the dead as in many primitive societies

a moment the birth of Christ, where eternity cuts into time

Passion of Christ, from the garden of Gethsemane to the hill of Calvary

Sacrifice of the Son of God on the Cross

no god modern atheism

Reason as in the eighteenth-century Enlightenment, the intellectual movement putting its faith in rational understanding as the means of obtaining knowledge and happiness

Race belief in racial superiorities (Hitler came to power the previous year, 1933)
Dialectic an ideology based on opposed social forces, as in Marxism

CHORUS IX   A plea for man's creativity to be used in the service of the Church

This Chorus presents the Church as mournful rather than joyful, and urges man to be creative, with four creative gifts specified for the service of God: sculpture, painting, music and word-making. These gifts join body and spirit, visible and invisible, which meet in the completion of the Church building, in physical light and metaphysical Light.

Of the four creative gifts specified in the second verse-paragraph, it is the last, the art of the wordsmith, that is (as might be expected) particularly relevant and interesting to the poet: out of 'verbal imprecisions' he is here striving for a 'perfect order' of words and the beauty of singing speech – the incantation of the Choruses themselves. Now Eliot does not deny the senses, and, as the **symbolic** church is completed by religious adornments, the light imagery that is to dominate the final Chorus breaks in.

Son ... the first three lines are entirely constructed from biblical phrases
House ... Sorrow a variation of Matthew 21:13 ('My house shall be called the house of prayer') to begin a description of the atmosphere in a typical church, contrasted with other public behaviour
communion of saints a phrase from the Apostles' Creed in the Book of Common Prayer
gifts to Your service a variation of the grace, 'Bless, O Lord, these gifts to our use and us to Thy service'
Visible and invisible a phrase from the Nicene Creed, applied here to man's dual (physical and spiritual) nature

CHORUS X   In praise of the built church, and of Light

Completed, the building is 'a visible church', a light in the darkness, and may lead on to 'the Visible Church' that could conquer the world. The wicked ways of the Devil must not be investigated; it is enough that the people have light. The mystical Light of God is then praised through lesser examples of light: sunrise, sunset, twilight, moonlight, starlight, and other lights in nature as well as various lights lit by us humans. We are quickly tired of light on earth, which we put out and relight continually, thanking God for shadow and darkness as well as giving thanks for His glory as the 'Light Invisible'.

In the light imagery of this concluding Chorus, the poet is not only using traditional biblical associations but imitating Dante in the final Canto of *Paradise*, of which Eliot remarked: 'Nowhere in poetry has experience so remote from ordinary experience been expressed so concretely, by a masterly use of that imagery of *light* which is the form of certain types of mystical experience.' By his imitation, Eliot also uses concrete visual images of a large range of types of light to suggest the spiritual, Invisible Light. Every part of this Chorus has reference to light, building to a climax: the first paragraph has the church as a light on a hill, the next the light of guidance for the believer, and then the great accumulation of lesser lights is brilliantly made to slow down and 'tire' at human tiring of light before the verse gathers momentum again towards the final ecstatic gratefulness. It concludes *Selected Poems* on a note of spiritual upliftment that is worlds away from the despair and disillusion of the earlier part of the volume.

light set on a hill a contraction of Christ's words in Matthew 5:14: 'Ye are the light of the world. A city that is set on a hill cannot be hid'

Iniquity of that 'great snake' Satan, whose ways the people are warned against probing too deeply

Good and Evil unlike in Choruses I and VII, suggesting the possible dangers of this knowledge if carried too far

O Light Invisible, we praise Thee! echoes 'O World invisible, we view thee', the opening of 'The Kingdom of God', by Francis Thompson (1859–1907); God as the 'Light of Light' is praised in the Nicene Creed

the less the lesser lights appear in the following lines: sunlight, moonlight, etcetera

light of altar ... sanctuary altar candles; and the light where the consecrated Host is reserved

we give Thee ... glory a version of a line in the Gloria, 'we give thanks to thee for thy great glory' (*Book of Common Prayer*)

PART THREE

CRITICAL APPROACHES

ALLUSIONS: BORROWING AND BETTERING

Anyone who looks through the notes in the Commentaries can hardly help observing how much Eliot owes to others, whether it is the words about the Magi from Bishop Andrewes or the Dantean detail of *The Hollow Men* and *Ash-Wednesday* or the biblical phrases in the final Choruses ... and so on. This may lead some readers to think less of Eliot, even to accuse him of stealing – an impression they may find reinforced when they discover whole books devoted to tracing his borrowings back to their sources.

Such an attitude would, however, be unjust to Eliot. It would unfairly deprive him of his due recognition as one of the most original poets ever to surprise the world. For Eliot transforms whatever he takes from others; he makes it distinctly his own. This is how he explained the process himself, in a defence of literary theft appropriately stolen from another critic, the French writer Rémy de Gourmont (1858–1915):

> One of the surest of tests is the way in which a poet borrows. Immature poets imitate; mature poets steal; bad poets deface what they take, and good poets make it into something better, or at least something different.

That is from the 1920 essay on the dramatist Philip Massinger (1583–1640) in *The Sacred Wood* (*Selected Essays*, p. 206). Thirty-six years later, in 'The Frontiers of Criticism', Eliot defined poetic originality as being largely 'an original way of assembling the most disparate and unlikely material to make a new whole' (*On Poetry and Poets*, Faber and Faber, 1957, p. 108).

Readers should remember such remarks when considering any of the poems where an accusation of plagiarism seems valid. It will invariably be found, on closer inspection, that Eliot has either improved or at least changed the original: by applying it in a new context, by altering words to show the original in a new light, by reworking it for his own poetic purposes, and above all by recasting different borrowings in wholly new combinations that are entirely his own.

Take the example of Jules Laforgue (1860–87), who gave Eliot a significant early impetus (see Background). What we have here is not an example of a lesser poet following in the footsteps of a greater, but an example of a major poet learning from and developing the work of a comparatively minor one as part of his own development. As Eliot saw it, he wanted to work out the implications of Laforgue after a period in which the young poet was taken over by the 'stronger personality' – that is, the more forcefully individual poetic identity – of the Frenchman. Laforgue himself did not live long enough to follow up his 'implications' in this way, and it has been pointed out, but perhaps not often enough, that Eliot cannot properly be called an imitator of Laforgue because, in the words of the American critic Edmund Wilson (1895–1972) in *Axel's Castle* (Charles Scribner's Sons, 1931), he is a 'superior artist ... more mature than Laforgue ever was' (Fontana, 1961, p. 85), with a 'perfect' workmanship that Laforgue rarely approached. Eliot's achievement was to take hints from Laforgue and turn them, with a sure mastery that was beyond Laforgue's capabilities, into images and **rhythms** that have become embedded in the minds of all who read modern poetry. Far from speaking with another's voice, he has found for himself a poetic voice that is totally distinct, totally original: as F.R. Leavis put it, in *New Bearings in English Poetry* (1932), to learn from Laforgue in the way that Eliot did 'is to be original to the point of genius' (Penguin, 1963, p. 69).

Much the same can be said even of Eliot's borrowings from Dante. For though that poet is, unlike Laforgue, not a lesser figure than Eliot himself, but a greater (Eliot put him on a level with Shakespeare), the use Eliot made of the Italian was also decisively directed towards his own unique vision – though 'decisively' seems the wrong word to use of a vision as tentative and exploratory as Eliot's spiritual search in the later poems; his modern hesitancy is in this way very different from Dante's medieval certainty, and no less poetically effective for that.

In short, Eliot knew exactly how to 'Make it New', in Ezra Pound's phrase. The 'it' might have been something found elsewhere: after all, literature is always concerned with many of the permanent subjects of human interest, such as time, love, reality and all the rest, crudely summed up by Sweeney (in the unfinished *Sweeney Agonistes*) as 'Birth, and copulation, and death'. An 'it' from any such central human topics is bound to have been treated countless times before. But Eliot used his genius to find a new angle, a new atmosphere, a new image or combination of images, a whole new poetic language to say things afresh. This is one reason why a continual chasing after sources has its dangers, and why it must be stressed that explanatory notes of the kind found in the Commentaries are not only no substitute for a reading of the poems themselves, but are also only first steps towards an understanding of the poems *as poetry* – as opposed to certain types of factual prose that have a definable, limited, objective, unambiguous meaning. As Eliot maintained, the explanation of literary works must not be mistaken for the understanding of such works: the idea that once a poem (or a novel, or a play) has been 'explained' then that is all we need to bother about. It is, of course, only the start of our response, and sometimes perhaps not even that: Eliot believed that we can respond to the poetry before we know very much about what the poem 'means'. What we do not want is to be left clutching the explanation alone, while the poetry has flown out of our grasp.

Eliot can both use a particular echo of another writer and make it into such a new thing that to track down the source is only one way of heading towards what the reader's most basic response needs to be, and it will not account for the power of the borrowing in a new context, or whether it is better or only different. The transformation of Eliot's borrowings may be found early and late, if perhaps less dramatically in the later verse than in the earlier. It may be useful to glance now at these 'early' and 'late' classifications, and how they affect critical views of Eliot's development.

DEVELOPMENT: PRE-CONVERSION AND POST-CONVERSION

This is a favourite way of dividing the poetry into what was published before and what was published after Eliot's reception into the Church of England. The works dating from beyond the end of *Selected Poems* (*Four Quartets* and the poetic dramas) fall into the second category, as does everything in *Selected Poems* after *The Hollow Men*, which is a kind of borderline marker.

In obvious ways, this distinction is true enough, and a helpful way of remembering certain characteristic differences between the two groups it forms. Even critics who insist most strongly on the underlying unity of Eliot's entire output have to face the fact that the man who wrote *Four Quartets* was a Christian and the man who wrote *The Waste Land* was not; that the lampooner of the Church in 'The Hippopotamus' was later to support it in his contributions to *The Rock*; that the satirist who mocked church wordiness in 'Mr Eliot's Sunday Morning Service' took church words reverently into 'A Song for Simeon'. What is more, the poet's later style – or perhaps one should say range of styles, for he never exactly repeated himself – is recognisably different from the earlier, so much so that many former admirers became critical and many of the formerly hostile became approving. In the same way, the overtly Christian themes indicated by titles such as *Ash-Wednesday* or 'Journey of the Magi' converted some Christians into readers of Eliot, just as they turned away unbelieving former readers who had found his earlier view of the world more to their taste.

All the same, two opposite things must be remembered about Eliot's work that the 'early' versus 'late', 'pre-conversion' versus 'post-conversion' division does not take into account: on the one hand, that there are more possible divisions than this; on the other, that Eliot progresses in a single curve as each new work evolves from what has gone before. There are further sub-divisions, within the early poems particularly, which are easily illustrated: look, for example, at the difference between the 'free' poems in *Prufrock and Other Observations* and the strict **quatrains** in *Poems 1920*. Eliot's evolving development is less easy to illustrate briefly, but some idea of it may be got from various approaches: following through the metamorphoses of Eliot's characteristic voices and *personae* from, say, Prufrock to Gerontion, Gerontion to Simeon; or noticing how 'Gerontion', for instance, was originally to be part of *The Waste Land*, bits left over from which in turn developed into *The Hollow Men*; or even looking back from the achieved vision in the later poems of acceptance to see how it had its origin in the implied quest for an alternative in the earlier poems of rejection.

Eliot's mastery of **versification** shows itself in the variety of verse forms to which he successfully turned his hand at different times. He exploits the possibilities of a form with considerable daring. For instance, even in his **quatrain** poems, with their given **rhymes** and **rhythms**, he breaks out of the form now and then to run over from one usually self-contained four-lined stanza into another. The two 'declinings' in 'Burbank with a Baedeker: Bleistein with a Cigar' are illustrations of this:

> The smoky candle end of time
>
> Declines.
>
> ...
>
> She entertains Sir Ferdinand
>
> Klein.

The high culture of the Canaletto and Mantegna paintings falls off sadly into the low modern civilisation represented by Bleistein; the acquired grandeur of the now titled upstart falls ludicrously at his delayed 'small' surname: it is all done by the versification. Another technique in the regularly rhymed poems is to use the compulsory rhymes themselves to make a point, as in the deliberately pathetic rhyme-words used in 'A Cooking Egg', where 'Sidney' collapses to 'kidney', or the 'trumpets', in a more tragic context, sink to 'crumpets'.

But even in his so-called 'free' verse, Eliot makes use of such devices, including rhyme. For '**free verse**', in Eliot, does not mean that rhyme is totally abandoned. On the contrary, Eliot saw that an irregular rhyme could be used – to greater effect than in much regularly rhymed verse – in a poem with a 'free' structure 'where rhyme is wanted for some special effect, for a sudden tightening-up, for a cumulative insistence, or for an abrupt change of mood' ('Reflections on *Vers Libre*', *To Criticize the Critic*, (Faber and Faber, 1965, p. 189).

- An example of a sudden tightening-up would be the end of 'Rhapsody on a Windy Night', where the aimless unrhymed detail of remembered routine is caught up by the constriction of the final cruel rhyme, itself also a 'last twist':

> 'The little lamp spreads a ring on the stair.
> Mount.

> The bed is open; the tooth-brush hangs on the wall,
> Put your shoes at the door, sleep, prepare for life.'

> The last twist of the knife.

- A cumulative insistence is usually achieved in Eliot's work by repeated words and phrases rather than rhymes, but in a passage like Part III of *Ash-Wednesday* the 'stair' rhymes and echoes mount with the ascending of the staircase: stair, (banister), air, (stairs ... wears), despair, stair, repair, stair, (hair ... hair), hair, stair, despair, stair.
- An abrupt change of mood is effected by the banal rhyme in 'Prufrock' where, after an ominous scene setting, we get the trivial ding-dong of

> In the room the women come and go
> Talking of Michelangelo.

However, 'Prufrock' has more rhymed than unrhymed lines, and it often happens in such poems that an *un*rhymed line signals a change, as in the striking interruption of 'No! I am not Prince Hamlet ...' after (floor-more; mean-screen; shawl-all ...) and before (do-two; tool-Fool ...) a series of rhymes, or as in the switch of mood at the final three unrhymed lines of the rhyming 'Preludes'.

It is remarkable how much, not how little, rhyme is used in *Selected Poems*. There are only two works in the whole book that do not at some stage use end-rhymes, 'Gerontion' and 'Journey of the Magi', the two works prominently using the prose sermons of Bishop Andrewes as stepping stones. ('Gerontion' also prominently uses other prose borrowings and imitates the unrhymed **blank verse** of the Jacobean dramatists.) Of course there are large unrhymed sections in the other works, particularly later, but all the others use rhyme at some stage. Even the almost totally unrhymed final Choruses break into rhyme now and then, as at the end of Chorus I (build-tilled, bread-bed ...) or the internal rhymes of 'What does the world say, does the whole world stray in high-powered cars on a by-pass way?' in Chorus VII. Yet the verse given to Gerontion and the Magus is just as 'poetic' in each case as it is anywhere else and uses many of the same techniques. 'Gerontion', for instance, employs **assonances** and **alliterations** that have much of the echoing and

welding effect of full rhyme: 'Blistered in Brussels, patched and peeled
…'; 'The woman keeps the kitchen, makes tea, / Sneezes at evening,
poking the peevish …'. And 'Journey of the Magi' uses Eliot's
characteristic later device of words repeated again and again as in
chanting, whether these are the significant words of the theme (birth,
death) or normally unimportant words like the 'and' that rhetorically piles
up the Magi's problems:

> Then the camel men cursing and grumbling
> And running away, and wanting their liquor and women,
> And the night-fires going out, and the lack of shelters,
> And the cities hostile and the towns unfriendly
> And the villages dirty and charging high prices:

That last quotation is also useful as an illustration of the fact that, as Eliot
said, 'Scansion tells us very little' ('Reflections on *Vers Libre*, *To Criticize
the Critic*, p. 185). Determined efforts have been made by various critics
to scan Eliot's verse, with diagrams showing where light syllables
alternate with stressed ones, and those who care to do so can mark and
count up the beats and the feet in any line they choose – but the
usefulness of such exercises is, unfortunately, very limited. In the lines
quoted, as everywhere else, any prosodic interest arises out of the
variations from an underlying norm. Even if one does not know that, say,
it is the departure from the prevailing two-syllable 'iambs' (unstressed
followed by stressed syllable) to the galloping three syllable 'anapaests'
(two unstressed syllables followed by a stressed one) that helps the
mounting effect of problem after problem, one can observe such an effect
– it helps to read aloud – without having to rely on complicated and
dubious prosodic jargon.

It is the same with rhymed lines: the **metrical** interest comes from
variation. Look how the second or rhyming lines have a different number
of syllables from the first, sometimes only slightly different, sometimes
prominently so, in the following passage from Part VI of *Ash-Wednesday*:

> And the lost heart stiffens and rejoices
> In the lost lilac and the lost sea voices
> And the weak spirit quickens to rebel
> For the bent golden-rod and the lost sea smell

> Quickens to recover
> The cry of quail and the whirling plover

We seem to be always on the verge of a steady **rhythmic** pattern, yet always the carpet is pulled from under our feet, jerking us into awareness. Eliot is following his own dictum (again in 'Reflections on *Vers Libre*', *To Criticize the Critic*, p. 185) that:

> the most interesting verse which has yet been written in our language has been done either by taking a very simple form, like the iambic pentameter, and constantly withdrawing from it, or taking no form at all, and constantly approximating to a very simple one. It is this contrast between fixity and flux, this unperceived evasion of monotony, which is the very life of verse.

Applying these observations to the poems will be found of great value to the student of Eliot's prosody. It needs no special knowledge, only an ear sensitive to rhythm.

Another of Eliot's dicta is that verse, whatever else it is, is a system of punctuation. Despite the concern he shows here, Eliot's practice has not always been thought to be as careful as it might have been. Look at that passage quoted from *Ash-Wednesday*, to find a momentary confusion about whether it is the spirit or the smell that 'Quickens to recover'. It is useful to remember that Eliot thought final commas were often unnecessary, as he himself always paused slightly at the end of a line of verse, but this does not help readers to see at once where the sense of a line runs on (as after 'rebel') and where it evidently breaks (as after 'smell'). There is a more serious instance in Part I of the same poem:

> And I pray that I may forget
> These matters that with myself I too much discuss
> Too much explain
> Because I do not hope to turn again
> Let these words answer
> For what is done, not to be done again
> May the judgement not be too heavy upon us

The lack of punctuation at the ends of the lines has here made it uncertain whether the 'Because ...' line goes with what precedes or follows it, or whether the 'For what is done' line completes the sense of the 'answer' in the previous line or leads on to 'May the judgement'.

Readers have to decide the punctuation for themselves, and it makes a difference whether they choose to put something like a full stop after 'turn again', or after 'answer', or after 'done again'.

Nor is punctuational confusion limited to the later, often lightly punctuated poems. There is a famous instance in the third stanza of 'Whispers of Immortality', which varies in punctuation from edition to edition: nothing after 'sense' and a comma after 'penetrate'; a semicolon after 'sense' and a comma after 'penetrate'; a comma after 'sense' and a semicolon after 'penetrate'. It is a useful exercise to see what effect on the meaning each change has. And, despite the irritation that some may feel, it is perhaps amusing that readers may accept the latest (third) punctuation as the most authoritative, or prefer an earlier one, or even suggest a fourth non-existent version (nothing after 'sense' and a semicolon after 'penetrate' might be the clearest) as the 'best' reading.

The developments in Eliot's prosody and punctuation from early to late are all part of larger developments, so it seems appropriate to set them in the following larger contexts.

STYLES & STRUCTURES

It has been pointed out that when one is looking for illustrations of different poetic styles, the most obvious thing is to set any other of Eliot's works against the controversial and influential **quatrain** poems, with their strict forms, their brilliant verbal wit, their sophistication, their frequently learned, ingenious, ironic, fantastical, superior, detached or unfeeling effects and tones. They are quite different from anything else, and so are convenient to employ in critical contrasts provided one does not forget the contrasts also possible within this group, or even within individual poems, as in the extraordinary changes of mood in 'A Cooking Egg' (and its extraordinary extra line) and in 'Sweeney Among the Nightingales'.

What is not so simple to show, and what has indeed never been very clearly shown, is the complex of differences between other poems from different periods. The crucial reason for this is that every time a distinction is made, an awareness of an essential similarity makes itself felt. In the same way, every time a similarity is asserted, an unignorable difference inconveniently raises its head. All the poetry bears the unmistakable imprint of a single poetic sensibility; at the same time, this poet never exactly repeated a poetic voice or manner that he had used earlier. So what we must aim at is a kind of double vision that can note differences in different periods and poems, while keeping an eye open for similarities.

Thus, Eliot is at his best in all periods when he is in some way dramatic. There is no poem in *Selected Poems* that does not in some way dramatise a situation or a mood. Even the most inward states exploit essentially dramatic external situations, as do the thinking voices from 'Prufrock', through 'Gerontion' and *The Hollow Men* to the final Choruses; even the most abstract concepts are given concrete life, as in the spiritual progress dramatised on the stairs in Part III of *Ash-Wednesday*, or the spiritual regression dramatised in the childhood scenes of *Animula*.

At the same time Eliot's startling earlier poems are more dramatic than lyrical, and his less startling later poems are more lyrical and meditative than dramatic. The difference can be seen by comparing, say,

> Now that lilacs are in bloom
> She has a bowl of lilacs in her room
> And twists one in her fingers while she talks.
> 'Ah, my friend, you do not know, you do not know
> What life is, you who hold it in your hands';
> (Slowly twisting the lilac stalks)
> 'You let it flow from you, you let it flow,
> And youth is cruel, and has no remorse
> And smiles at situations which it cannot see.'
> I smile, of course,
> And go on drinking tea. ('Portrait of a Lady')

and

> Blown hair is sweet, brown hair over the mouth blown,
> Lilac and brown hair;
> Distraction, music of the flute, stops and steps of the
>   mind over the third stair,
> Fading, fading; strength beyond hope and despair
> Climbing the third stair. (*Ash Wednesday*, Part III)

There are remarkable similarities here, from the characteristically regretful use of lilac to the **rhymes** at the end of lines of varying length. But the repetitions in 'Portrait of a Lady' are not used to the same end as the repetitions in *Ash-Wednesday*: 'you do not know, you do not know' is not a foreshadowing of, but in another poetic world from, 'Because I do not hope to know ... Because I know I shall not know' (Part I) – for the simple reason that the lady's affectedness is being mocked, while the twistings and turnings of the convert are anything but mocked. Her sexual longings are made pathetic; his are felt with tragic intensity. In the first case the repetitions underline what is pitiable and contribute humorous satirical exaggeration; in the other the repetitions provide a lyrical note of yearning that is purely sympathetic. And of course nowhere in *Ash-Wednesday* is there anything remotely like the casually cruel demolition job of

> I smile, of course,
> And go on drinking tea.

Then there is **versification**. Eliot uses a number of different types throughout, but the greatest variety is found in the earlier work. There we have the rhymed speech-**rhythm**, the unstressed unwindings of 'Prufrock' (Let us go then, you and I, /When the evening is spread out against the sky') or the 'Portrait':

> The October night comes down; returning as before
> Except for a slight sensation of being ill at ease
> I mount the stairs and turn the handle of the door
> And feel as if I had mounted on my hands and knees.

immediately followed by the rhymed beat-rhythm, the stressed definition of 'Preludes':

> His soul stretched tight across the skies
> That fade behind a city block,
> Or trampled by insistent feet
> At four and five and six o'clock;

Or we can contrast the unrhymed **blank verse** effects of 'Gerontion' with the regularly rhymed 'fixed' structures following it in *Selected Poems*, or with the irregularly rhymed 'organic' structures which precede it.

The differences are more striking than the similarities in these early works, culminating in *The Waste Land*. When we turn to the later works, however, the similarities are more noticeable than the differences. Even what look at first sight like obvious changes of direction within a poem usually turn out to be sharing the same tempo and mood as the rest, as when Eliot's version of the Litany of the Virgin Mary ('Lady of silences'), with its short lines on the page, is essentially close to the endlessly circling lines of the rest of *Ash-Wednesday*: 'End of the endless / Journey to no end / Conclusion of all that / Is inconclusible / Speech without word and / Word of no speech' (Part II) is more like than unlike 'Against the Word the unstilled world still whirled / About the centre of the silent Word' (Part V).

There is a feeling that the characteristic later verse forms have taken Eliot right out of the reach of conventional prosody: earlier one feels he is reacting against established forms by twisting them into new shapes; later one feels he is creating his own forms, following his own rules rather than breaking the rules of others. It is largely a matter of the prevailing rhythm.

Again, Eliot in all periods displays great **rhythmic** variety, both from poem to poem and within individual poems. But his rhythms are typically more varied and energetic before *The Hollow Men,* and more relaxed and repetitive after that. The greatest range of rhythmic vitality and variation is found in *The Waste Land,* but almost any other section of the earlier work provides more of this range than can be found in the later. The early range includes such juxtapositions as incantatory, prophet-in-the-wilderness Prufrock letting his biblical rhetoric fall through swift rhythmic gradations to self-deprecatory, please-don't-bother Prufrock of the easy-going phrase:

> But though I have wept and fasted, wept and prayed,
> Though I have seen my head (grown slightly bald)
>> brought in upon a platter,
> I am no prophet – and here's no great matter;

It also includes such combinations as the excited entrance of Sir Ferdinand moving ambiguously to the melancholy meditations of Burbank:

>> Lights, lights,
> She entertains Sir Ferdinand

Klein. Who clipped the lion's wings
  And flea'd his rump and pared his claws?
Thought Burbank, meditating on
  Time's ruins, and the seven laws.

The later poems do not characteristically exhibit this kind of rapid shifting. This is not to say the later poems are less good, only that their characteristic method is different. This method uses incantatory **rhythms** that repeat over and again the words and phrases that the poet is meditatively exploring:

If the lost word is lost, if the spent word is spent
If the unheard, unspoken
Word is unspoken, unheard;
Still is the unspoken word, the Word unheard,
The Word without a word, ... (*Ash-Wednesday*, Part V)

This is the opposite of the early verse, where the speed and complexity of the changes, with the associated concision, demand great alertness on the part of the reader. Here, we find instead an expansion and general loosening-up.

This loosening-up is seen in the structures of the later verse, in both the smaller and the larger units. In the case of the larger units of complete poems, Eliot's method of composition, joining up bits to form new wholes, seems to have contributed to the impression of occasionally over-extended conglomerations. This is perhaps more noticeable in the later poems, where some assemblages, despite all the similarities of tone and texture, seem to lack the earlier air of tightly-knit inevitability, despite all the variety. It may be relevant to note that poems like 'Prufrock' and *The Waste Land* were reduced to their present form from larger structures, whereas poems like *The Hollow Men* and *Ash-Wednesday* grew from shorter, separate structures. Certainly, in the smaller units of phrases, sentences and paragraphs, we find the economy and urgency of lines like:

The tiger springs in the new year. Us he devours.
  Think at last
We have not reached conclusion, when I
Stiffen in a rented house. ('Gerontion')

largely abandoned for the less concentrated, gentler flux and reflux of thought:

> Will the veiled sister pray for
> Those who walk in darkness, who chose thee and oppose
>   thee,[?]
>
> ...
>
>   Will the veiled sister pray
> For children at the gate
> Who will not go away and cannot pray:
> Pray for those who chose and oppose[?] (*Ash-Wednesday*, Part V)

The repetitive, looser quality of the later poems is mirrored by their characteristic imagery, which is vaguer, more dreamlike and beautiful than the characteristically striking, realistic, precise earlier imagery. Where the earlier style of writing brings off audacious feats with its sordid city images and perpetually surprising combinations of words, the later style turns to nature and almost always avoids upsetting the prevailing mood of thoughtful deliberation by any very startling change of direction in either imagery or sentence-structure. The personal trademarks of street and suchlike images are left behind when the poet adapts the images found in older traditions, such as the rose of medieval allegory, the Garden of Paradise, the biblical desert.

IMAGERY

It is a rewarding exercise to go through Eliot's poetry looking for recurrences of images, noting any developments as well as repetitions. Nothing else can more helpfully and easily bring out the poet's enduring concerns and the overall links between each part of the larger work formed by his total output. We are concerned here only with *Selected Poems,* but the principle holds good for that whole, as well as the larger totality.

The images that recur are of many kinds. The American critic Leonard Unger has made a useful list of some of the most prominent ones, in 'T.S. Eliot's Images of Awareness' (*T.S. Eliot: The Man and His Work,* ed. Allen Tate, Chatto and Windus, 1967, pp. 205–6), and a list like this is an excellent place for the interested student to begin: flowers and gardens; water; times of year (months and seasons) and times of day; smoke and fog; city streets; human parts, including hair; stairs; music; smell.

Flower and *garden* images have been frequently pointed out, particularly the spring flowers, hyacinth and lilac, at times of yearning remembrance, the use of trees, and the juxtaposition of garden images with *desert* ones. Whereas the *wasteland* images are barren, waiting for rain, the desert has a dual role: sterile, but a place of spiritual renewal. Remember that the evergreen yew, which began as a **symbol** of immortality, became associated with *death* by its constant use in graveyards: Eliot uses it in both ways. Other death images that can have dual associations are *bones,* as in *Ash-Wednesday,* though in the earlier poems bones are used mainly for their negative associations, emphasised by their frequent placing next to *rats* (as three times in *The Waste Land*). The groups of *animal* images (such as ape, fox, dog, cat – including tiger, jaguar and leopard) are used mainly for threatening effects, in poems as different as 'Sweeney Among the Nightingales' and *Animula.* This will lead on to other creatures like *birds* ... at which point, its range of possible additions having been demonstrated, the given list can be resumed.

The most striking *water* images, apart from the situations where water is lacking in the dry land and where the desiccated wait for an often spiritual rain, are the *sea* images, which occur at particularly moving moments of recollection and revelation in poems as various as 'Prufrock', 'Gerontion', 'Burbank ...', *Ash-Wednesday* and 'Marina'.

Times of year and day are used for their emotional resonances so regularly that it is only in some of the **quatrain** poems that no examples will strike the attentive reader. The spring (April to May) is used not simply as a conventional image of joyous renewal but as a 'cruel' reminder; and the use of 'twilight', intermediate times of day, for uncertain, intermediate states. *Smoke* and *fog* are usually part of the complex of images from *city streets* and modern life generally, though there is a notably different use of fog in 'Marina'.

Arms, hands and fingers, legs and feet, heads and eyes are all examples of *human parts* used prominently by Eliot to stand for people and direct our feelings. Perhaps the most powerful of such images is the human hair occurring in 'Prufrock', *The Waste Land*, and *Ash-Wednesday*.

Stairs are chiefly associated with the sexually troubled, whether it is the narrator's worry about women at the top of the stairs ('Prufrock', 'Portrait'), or the lack of a woman ('Rhapsody'), or the loss of a woman ('Burbank ...'), or a dead relationship with a woman (*The Waste Land*), or the renunciation of women (*Ash-Wednesday*). The climbing of stairs is therefore difficult, morally and emotionally, even for the saints who mount their symbolic stair in 'A Song for Simeon'.

Eliot's interest in *music* is seen in such titles as 'Preludes', 'Rhapsody on a Windy Night', 'A Song for Simeon', and *Four Quartets*, where this interest culminates. 'Portrait of a Lady' uses musical motifs throughout, and lesser instances may be found in many other poems.

Finally, the use of *smell* is an enduring characteristic of Eliot's imagery, from all those early (and especially female) smells, encountered in streets and drawing-rooms ('Rhapsody' has a long list), to the smells of flowers encountered early and late.

THEMES & VARIATIONS

The imagery a poet uses is one way he gives life to his themes. The themes that Eliot explores in *Selected Poems* can be followed up by the student (with the help of the Commentaries, as needed) in much the same way as the imagery can be, and at the same time. For the types of images chosen by the poet will help in indicating aspects of his themes.

Typical themes in Eliot grow out of answering two related questions: How do we live? and How should we live? The answer to the first question predominates in the early poems, which typically examine the nature of the wasteland within individual modern lives and show how such lives are barely 'lived' at all: the theme of the unlived life, of timid withdrawal from life, is significant here. This early answer is a largely descriptive answer; it does not provide much in the way of alternatives to the prevailing sterility. The answer to the second question rises out of the first answer and predominates in the later poems, which typically examine the spiritual needs of the wastelanders and suggest what must be done to make the desert bloom: here the ascetic theme of renunciation, of dying to the old life to be born into the new, becomes important. Though this later answer is largely prescriptive, only at times in the final Choruses does the poetry smack of blatant religious propaganda: more usually, everything is too tentative and exploratory and wondering to be labelled didactic and exhortatory.

Some important themes are related to time. For example, in *Selected Poems* many variations are played on the theme of the relationship of past to present, telling a story of decay by juxtaposing the glorious ancients and the inglorious moderns (as in Prufrock and Michelangelo or John the Baptist or Hamlet, the 'Lady' and Juliet, Burbank and Mark Antony, Sweeney's girl and Ariadne or Nausicaa), but also deromanticising figures from the past to show that their human frailty is essentially shared with ours (as in Agamemnon, the Roman legionaries, the Magi, Simeon). Later in *Selected Poems* the significance of the birth of Christ (the Incarnation), a moment both in time and out of it (in eternity), is an important development of a 'time' theme that will be taken further in *Four Quartets*.

Other large themes that might be pursued through *Selected Poems* include: appearance and reality, the actual and the ideal, the quest, the nature of belief, suffering, salvation, good and evil, the links between art and life.

To conclude, here are three general observations about *Selected Poems* that point to both the enduring interests of the poet and the enduring interest that the poetry holds for readers. Firstly, there is the persistence in the memory, as in the poems, of certain characters like Sweeney; like his opposite, Prufrock (the 'Prufrockian' persona is adapted in several other characters, such as the narrator of 'Portrait', Gerontion, Burbank, the narrator of *The Hollow Men* and Simeon); like the sinister Jews; and like the women, who are often made to seem either rather repulsive at close quarters, or unattainably remote and idealised. Secondly, it is remarkable how personal Eliot's poetry is, despite all his insistence on the impersonality of art and on the strict need to separate the man who suffers from the mind which creates. He learnt from Laforgue how to utilise personal problems in poetry, and the special

interest his poetry provides as a sort of autobiography of mental and
spiritual breakdown and recovery is not at all easy to deny. Thirdly, only
prudery could prevent readers from recognising the fact that the personal
theme that most persistently underlies Eliot's poetry is sexual: it may be
intellectualised or disguised or impersonalised, but the erotic note, as
sounded in frustration, disappointment, disgust, regret and longing,
insistently recurs.

Extended Commentaries

TEXT 1   PORTRAIT OF A LADY

Thou hast committed –
Fornication: but that was in another country,
And besides, the wench is dead.
    The Jew of Malta

I

Among the smoke and fog of a December afternoon
You have the scene arrange itself – as it will seem to do –
With 'I have saved the afternoon for you';
And four wax candles in the darkened room,
Four rings of light upon the ceiling overhead,
An atmosphere of Juliet's tomb
Prepared for all the things to be said, or left unsaid.
We have been, let us say, to hear the latest Pole
Transmit the Preludes, through his hair and finger-tips.
'So intimate, this Chopin, that I think his soul
Should be resurrected only among friends
Some two or three, who will not touch the bloom
That is rubbed and questioned in the concert room.'
– And so the conversation slips
Among velleities and carefully caught regrets
Through attenuated tones of violins
Mingled with remote cornets
And begins.
'You do not know how much they mean to me, my friends,
And how, how rare and strange it is, to find
In a life composed so much, so much of odds and ends,
(For indeed I do not love it ... you knew? you are not
    blind!
How keen you are!)

To a friend who has these qualities,
Who has, and gives
Those qualities upon which friendship lives.
How much it means that I say this to you –
Without these friendships – life, what *cauchemar!*'

   Among the windings of the violins
And the ariettes
Of cracked cornets
Inside my brain a dull tom-tom begins
Absurdly hammering a prelude of its own,
Capricious monotone
That is at least one definite 'false note'.
– Let us take the air, in a tobacco trance,
Admire the monuments,
Discuss the late events,
Correct our watches by the public clocks.
Then sit for half an hour and drink our bocks.

                    II

   Now that lilacs are in bloom
She has a bowl of lilacs in her room
And twists one in her finger while she talks.
'Ah, my friend, you do not know, you do not know
What life is, you who hold it in your hands';
(Slowly twisting the lilac stalks)
'You let it flow from you, you let it flow,
And youth is cruel, and has no remorse
And smiles at situations which it cannot see.'
I smile, of course,
And go on drinking tea.

   'Yet with these April sunsets, that somehow recall
My buried life, and Paris in the Spring,
I feel immeasurably at peace, and find the world
To be wonderful and youthful, after all.'

The voice returns like the insistent out-of-tune
Of a broken violin on an August afternoon:
'I am always sure that you understand
My feelings, always sure that you feel,
Sure that across the gulf you reach your hand.

You are invulnerable, you have no Achilles' heel.
You will go on, and when you have prevailed
You can say: at this point many a one has failed.
But what have I, but what have I, my friend,
To give you, what can you receive from me?
Only the friendship and the sympathy
Of one about to reach her journey's end.

I shall sit here, serving tea to friends ....'

I take my hat: how can I make cowardly amends
For what she has said to me?
You will see me any morning in the park
Reading the comics and the sporting page.
Particularly I remark
An English countess goes upon the stage.
A Greek was murdered at a Polish dance,
Another bank defaulter has confessed.
I keep my countenance,
I remain self-possessed
Except when a street-piano, mechanical and tired
Reiterates some worn-out common song
With the smell of hyacinths across the garden
Recalling things that other people have desired.
Are these ideas right or wrong?

III

The October night comes down; returning as before
Except for a slight sensation of being ill at ease
I mount the stairs and turn the handle of the door

And feel as if I had mounted on my hands and knees.
'And so you are going abroad; and when do you return?
But that's a useless question.
You hardly know when you are coming back,
You will find so much to learn.'
My smile falls heavily among the bric-à-brac.

'Perhaps you can write to me.'
My self-possession flares up for a second;
This is as I had reckoned.
'I have been wondering frequently of late
(But our beginnings never know our ends!)
Why we have not developed into friends.'
I feel like one who smiles, and turning shall remark
Suddenly, his expression in a glass.
My self-possession gutters; we are really in the dark.

'For everybody said so, all our friends,
They all were sure our feelings would relate
So closely! I myself can hardly understand.
We must leave it now to fate.
You will write, at any rate.
Perhaps it is not too late.
I shall sit here, serving tea to friends.'

And I must borrow every changing shape
To find expression ... dance, dance
Like a dancing bear,
Cry like a parrot, chatter like an ape.
Let us take the air, in a tobacco trance –

Well! and what if she should die some afternoon,
Afternoon grey and smoky, evening yellow and rose;
Should die and leave me sitting pen in hand
With the smoke coming down above the housetops;
Doubtful, for a while
Not knowing what to feel or if I understand

Or whether wise or foolish, tardy or too soon …
Would she not have the advantage, after all?
This music is successful with a 'dying fall'
Now that we talk of dying –
And should I have the right to smile?

The themes of 'Portrait of a Lady' apply at least as much to the young man who narrates the poem as to its ostensible subject. Both are victims of their different feelings, which hold them prisoner in different ways. This is essentially a poem about trapped, frustrated lives. This does not mean they are viewed only in a tragic light: on the contrary, they are also exposed to some withering humour on Eliot's part. This dual aspect, which is reflected throughout in the themes these lives embody – of entrapment versus escape, of affectation versus genuine values, of shrinking from life versus trying to face up to its demands, of self-assurance and superiority versus self-doubt and guilt – makes each of them tragi-comic.

The 'lady' can be seen as tragic when we as readers begin to realise her deep emotional needs by the middle of the poem, where she sits twisting the lilacs and recalling her youth in an eloquent appeal for friendship. However, before this we have been made to laugh at her affectations, especially her ludicrous speech, with its soulful delicacies and 'carefully caught regrets' and exaggerated repetitions, but also such details as the 'four wax candles in the darkened room' that set the scene for this elderly Juliet's encounter with her latest young man.

This young man also presents himself, through the **monologue** the poet gives him, in a way that shows him in different lights. While his critical attitude to the lady (underlined by a satirical use of music that can juxtapose, say, Chopin preludes and a drumming headache) lays him open to criticism for implied superiority and even callousness, he does give us – again in the central section – a picture of himself that is a comically-observed piece of self-mockery, also showing us he is sensitive, and a victim – trapped by his own view of himself. Though he has affected an attitude of amused condescension to the lady, doubts begin to enter his mind as to whether his ideas are 'right or wrong'; feelings of guilt begin to assail his stronghold. This is well caught in his frequent smiles, which may be supercilious or disarming, self-assured or distressed as he tries to respond to the lady's repeated demands for his 'friendship' to brighten her nightmare existence, but which come to an end with his wondering what 'right' he has to smile at her in the first place. He is perhaps a more tragic figure than she is after all: for he is a timid shrinker from life, one who needs to escape from feeling into trivial routine, whereas the lady, for all her pretentiousness, does at least have her strongly-felt needs and values.

All the same, as the lady seems to triumph with her successful 'music' of high culture and true feeling, so the young man has developed into awareness, not only of the lady's 'advantage' over him, but also of himself. This self-awareness makes him ultimately the main subject of the **monologue**, the evolving of this self-knowledge its main theme.

These thematic concerns are reflected in the imagery, and the images that immediately strike the reader are the musical ones, which appear in each of the three parts of the poem. These musical motifs help to link the sections and, by recalling previous uses of music in the poem, can be used to evoke and comment on moods and memories that have previously been established. Perhaps this is one reason why the first section (which has to do the establishing) contains more examples of musical images than the other two sections (with more repetitions, just as in the repeated phrases of ordinary music), as if to prepare the reader for a 'musical' use of words, letting the technique of repetition with variation add its effects to the evolving sequence.

As with most of the imagery in this poem, the musical images are used initially in a satirical way; it is only later that ambivalent emotions creep in. The piano-playing of 'the latest Pole', transmitting Chopin through his hair as well as his fingers, suggests an affectedly 'spiritual' artistic sensitivity matching that of the lady herself, as she gushes into speech about the composer's 'soul' and his 'bloom', as of a delicate exotic fruit, which is rubbed off by the common public at concerts. This paralleling of music and affectation continues with the explicit linking of the rarefied genteel conversation with the gentle music of ethereal violins and distant cornets – humorously underlined by the pun on 'composed' to describe the lady's life. This first section ends with a reappearance of the violins and cornets, 'winding' or performing elegant 'ariettes' in a way that echoes the lady's elegant repetitiveness – which in turn starts his own one-note 'tom-tom' prelude beating in the young narrator's brain, 'one definite "false note'" to give him a headache and make him long to escape. In the second part, however, repeated instances of music do not only irritate the young man ('the insistent out-of-tune / Of a broken violin'; 'a street piano, mechanical and tired / Reiterates some worn-out common song'), they also demonstrate the power of the most undistinguished music to evoke memories, to invest commonplace recollections with a new strength of feeling – and therefore, as unhappy reminders, to make him lose his self-possession and experience his first doubts. This takes us through to the third section where, though he remembers having to dance to the lady's tune like some trained bear, it is her higher feelings that still pursue him: her 'music' still triumphantly sounds in his mind's ear, for all the affected melancholy shown by the Shakespearian 'dying fall'.

Whereas the musical images help to unite the parts of the poem, Eliot's seasonal imagery distinguishes the different times of year in which the different events of the poem occur. Darkness characterises the late months of the outer sections; sun and flowers characterise the middle section. So the initial 'smoke and fog of a December afternoon' of the first visit to the lady is set against the central April sunsets and lilacs, spring images of the lady's longings and her revived memories of the youthful past of 'My buried life, and Paris in the Spring'. During this spring visit, however, the lady's irritating speech reminds the young man of an irritating violin heard in the heat of high summer; and it is not until he has escaped that the smell of more spring flowers (hyacinths) combine with music to make him think of the desires of people like the lady, and wonder if his critical attitude is the right one. The third visit finds darkness again in the descending October night, but when the narrator thinks of the lady's future death, it seems as if her spring sunsets ('yellow and rose') alleviate the 'grey and smoky' afternoon of her imagined day of death – another victory for the lady?

Other uses of imagery include the candle images, in the four candles to indicate and mock the lady's exquisite sensibility and enhance the 'atmosphere of Juliet's tomb' as well as in the candle-flame metaphors used to present the young man's self-possession as it 'flares up' and then 'gutters'. But the most notable remaining images are those of entrapment and the resulting wish to escape, which is a central concern of the poem. Both the lady and the narrator she wishes to make her 'friend' are imprisoned in different ways and are looking for a means of breaking out. The lady's drawing-room, described as a tomb, is a place where she endlessly serves tea, surrounded by the claustrophobic clutter of her bric-à-brac. It is little wonder that the young man feels uneasy about returning, and that to climb the stairs to this imprisoning room is seen as a penitential activity ('as if I had mounted on my hands and knees'): at the top he will be ensnared by feelings of guilt, at the least. The prison atmosphere is made more constricting by the many repetitions – the tea, the smiles, the lady's dozen uses of 'friend' – and is finally focused on the images of the captive animals, the dancing bear, the crying parrot and the chattering ape, used as a grotesque comment on the lady's high culture that the young man feels bound to imitate. He wants to escape from this stifling indoor atmosphere to outdoor freedom from the clutching intimacies of the lady. There the complementary images are of air ('Let us take the air') and the 'tobacco trance' of soothing cigarettes, together with a drink of beer rather than tea.

It is in the park, however, that the narrator most freely presents an image of himself as both ridiculous and sad; and it is here that we first realise he is tied down as much by his own view of himself as by the demands put upon him by the lady. Out in the park he is just as trapped inside himself as when aping her ways and bearing with her emotional appeals in the drawing-room. The painter of this portrait turns out to be weighed down by heavier chains than even its subject. Both are victims of a paralysing way of life, but at the end of the poem she will still have the whip-hand over him – in his own mind.

TEXT 2   SWEENEY AMONG THE NIGHTINGALES

Apeneck Sweeney spreads his knees
Letting his arms hang down to laugh,
The zebra stripes along his jaw
Swelling to maculate giraffe.

The circles of the stormy moon
Slide westward toward the River Plate,

Death and the Raven drift above
And Sweeney guards the hornèd gate.

Gloomy Orion and the Dog
Are veiled; and hushed the shrunken seas;
The person in the Spanish cape
Tries to sit on Sweeney's knees

Slips and pulls the table cloth
Overturns a coffee-cup,
Reorganised upon the floor
She yawns and draws a stocking up;

The silent man in mocha brown
Sprawls at the window-sill and gapes;
The waiter brings in oranges
Bananas figs and hothouse grapes;

The silent vertebrate in brown
Contracts and concentrates, withdraws:
Rachel *née* Rabinovitch
Tears at the grapes with murderous paws;

She and the lady in the cape
Are suspect, thought to be in league;
Therefore the man with heavy eyes
Declines the gambit, shows fatigue,

Leaves the room and reappears
Outside the window, leaning in,
Branches of wistaria
Circumscribe a golden grin;

The host with someone indistinct
Converses at the door apart,
The nightingales are singing near
The Convent of the Sacred Heart,

And sang within the bloody wood
When Agamemnon cried aloud,
And let their liquid siftings fall
To stain the stiff dishonoured shroud.

It was suggested in the Commentaries that in this poem 'power' rises above 'puzzle', which is perhaps not the case with all the poems in the 1920 volume. Some critics, however, have found the element of 'puzzle' so strong in this poem that it interferes with their enjoyment and appreciation. Hugh Kenner says it exhibits 'Eliot's besetting vice, a never wholly penetrable ambiguity about what is supposed to be happening' (*The Invisible Poet: T.S. Eliot,* W.H. Allen, 1960, p. 79), and he is echoed even more forcefully by Malcolm Pittock, who maintains that the voice narrating the poem 'does not know what the hell is going on' (*Essays in Criticism,* 300, 1980, p. 34). Such reactions are easily understandable, and it would be futile to allege there is no truth in them, as most readers have to agree that, whatever the speaker of the poem may know or not know, *they* do not know what is supposed to be going on.

Is it entirely a cop-out to suggest that this puzzle is part of the power of the poem? When we recall that Eliot declared a 'sense of foreboding' was all he consciously set out to create in the poem, we can more easily recognise how, because fear can be increased by ignorance, increased uncertainty and ambivalence and obscurity can add to what is frightening. The sense of foreboding, therefore, is enhanced as the questions we ask accumulate. Is Sweeney in danger of being killed, or only of being seduced or robbed by the prostitutes 'thought to be in league'? *Are* they in league? Are they even prostitutes? Eliot said the setting was a 'dive', defined by the *Oxford English Dictionary* as a 'disreputable place of resort', and it is certainly given an air of unrespectability, but is it more than a 'low' drinking-den? Is the man in brown a soldier recently returned from the First World War, or just dressed in brown civilian clothes? What is the significance, if any, either way? Is he the same as the man 'with heavy eyes', or is the latter another man who also withdraws from the room? This same man is thought to be *Sweeney* by at least one commentator, adding to the possibilities for confusion; yet it seems an unlikely reading, as the *isolation* of Sweeney is a major factor in the build-up of tension. But is the 'someone indistinct', with whom the host converses 'apart', an assassin or hit-man, or another 'innocent' bystander, or what?

The answers to these questions depend on individual readers and how much or how little they are prepared to 'read things into' or 'draw things out of' the poem, and especially on how the major linkage in the poem is interpreted: the relation implied in the poem between Sweeney and Agamemnon, as the final stanza moves right away from the low den of the present to the 'bloody wood' in ancient Greece. The linking of the uncertainly apprehended modern events with a very certainly known murder of antiquity, gives stronger evidence for another plotted murder, this time of Sweeney, and retrospectively heightens the 'murderous' message of Rachel's 'paws'. It could, however, be taken as merely another occasion when Eliot, in making a contrast between the anciently grand and noble and the modernly sordid and pathetic, has shown up some trivial modern scene of betrayal by ironic contrast with a serious ancient one. There is the undeniable presence of aspects of this typical contrast of sordid present and heroic past, but this time there is a strangely moving link established between Sweeney and the equally human and 'maculate' Agamemnon.

Here it is chiefly the presence of the nightingales, singing now as well as then, that suggests a closer rather than a looser identification between Sweeney and Agamemnon. In *The Waste Land*, nightingales are associated with rape and seduction, and it may be that here those **symbols** of betrayal combine with the slang sense of nightingales as prostitutes to indicate Sweeney's downfall will be sexual, and maybe not fatal; but Agamemnon's betrayal was sexual *and* fatal, as he was murdered by his wife and her lover, and the transition from Sweeney's situation to the king's is notable for both its smoothness and its seriousness. Even the choice of 'The Convent of the Sacred Heart' for the present-day nightingales underlines the seriousness of the transition to their olden-day location of the 'bloody wood', with no suggestion that the one is ridiculous in juxtaposition with the other.

As for the other links that weld the poem together, they include such things as the characteristic sexual possibilities of certain phrases such as 'spreads his knees', 'hornèd gate', 'vertebrate ... withdraws', or the chosen fruits, and the eerie imagery (the moon, the sea, the wood, and so on) that is also so often animal: not only the prominent nightingale motifs, but the ape, zebra and giraffe attributes of Sweeney, the evil omens of Raven and Dog (always menacing in Eliot), the man seen as merely 'vertebrate', Rachel's 'paws'.

Above all, the unifying momentum within the poem – with increasing tension as the ominous details and uncertainties mount up – is maintained by the **versification**, particularly in the thirty-two lines forming the one long third and final sentence, with each stanza either running on to the next or separated by no more than commas or semicolons. This makes for an extraordinarily powerful crescendo towards the dramatic climax of the poem at the very end. The strict **rhyme** scheme (a-b-c-b) and consistent **metrical** pattern (tetrameter, or four feet per line) of the **quatrains** (stanzas of four lines) sit oddly at variance with the disorderly goings on in the 'dive', but may serve to underline that disorderliness by their orderly framework containing it. At any rate, they unquestionably fit the final two stanzas, described by perhaps the only other poet who could challenge Eliot's pre-eminence in the twentieth century, W.B. Yeats (1865–1939), in the Introduction to his *Oxford Book of Modern Verse* (Oxford University Press, 1936, p. xxii), as the only ones in Eliot's early work that 'speak in the great manner' – meaning the manner of Yeats himself. But the juxtaposition and changes of tone and perspective involved here are, in the context of the whole poem, uniquely Eliot's own.

The very last line – 'To stain the stiff dishonoured shroud' – may well point out the echo of 'dim / Dishonoured brow', from 'Ichabod' (translates 'the glory has departed'), a poem by John Greenleaf Whittier (1807–92) about the American politician Daniel Webster (1782–1852), which supports the theme of betrayal already presented in the murder of Agamemnon, and paralleled by the intrigue against Sweeney. This sort of information can be helpful to the reader, if only by indicating certain reinforcing themes that could be followed up. But it is obvious that the essence of the line can only be extracted by reference to both the context of the line and its own impact, with the **alliterated** hissing sounds, and particularly the repeated 'st', imitating the bird droppings splattering on the sheet covering the dead man, where they probably add to the stiffness already caused by his dried blood and rigor mortis – and certainly add, even if only figuratively, to the dishonour of that death, which has in turn led some critics to see a connection with sleepy Sweeney and suggest a 'wet dream' as the source of his dishonourable stain … Where does one stop? Some interpretations have to be ruled out, as a line that means anything and everything is meaningless. But this cannot alter the fact that no source-citing is going to exhaust such a line of its possible resonances; nor can it account for the new impact, in a new context, of such borrowings.

TEXT 3   MARINA

> *Quis hic locus, quae*
> *regio, quae mundi plaga?*

What seas what shores what grey rocks and what islands
What water lapping the bow
And scent of pine and the woodthrush singing through
    the fog
What images return
O my daughter.

Those who sharpen the tooth of the dog, meaning
Death
Those who glitter with the glory of the hummingbird,
    meaning
Death
Those who sit in the sty of contentment, meaning
Death
Those who suffer the ecstasy of the animals, meaning
Death

Are become unsubstantial, reduced by a wind,
A breath of pine, and the woodsong fog
By this grace dissolved in place

What is this face, less clear and clearer
The pulse in the arm, less strong and stronger –

> Given or lent? more distant than stars and nearer than
>   the eye
>
> Whispers and small laughter between leaves and
>   hurrying feet
> Under sleep, where all the waters meet.
>
> Bowsprit cracked with ice and paint cracked with heat.
> I made this, I have forgotten
> And remember.
> The rigging weak and the canvas rotten
> Between one June and another September.
> Made this unknowing, half conscious, unknown, my own.
> The garboard strake leaks, the seams need caulking.
> This form, this face, this life
> Living to live in a world of time beyond me; let me
> Resign my life for this life, my speech for that unspoken,
> The awakened, lips parted, the hope, the new ships.
>
> What seas what shores what granite islands towards
>   my timbers
> And woodthrush calling through the fog
> My daughter.

The title and the **epigraph** react against one another, effecting what Eliot described as a 'crisscross': the revealed truth in Shakespeare's play is wonderful, as Pericles discovers his supposedly dead daughter is in fact alive; in contrast, the revealed truth in Seneca's is horrific, as Hercules discovers he has, in a fit of madness, killed his children. Each acts as a comment on the other, and a balanced tension results – especially when it is not the Shakespearian but the grimly frenzied Senecan rhetoric, with its list of questions ('What place is this, what region, what part of the world?'), that seems to be taken up in the first lines of the poem: 'What seas what shores what grey rocks and what islands / What water ... / What images return ...'. Some readers take these as questions, as in Seneca, but they end with a full stop (as again at the conclusion of the poem), and are not so much questions as statements of wonder. It is like the difference between 'What memories do I have?' and 'What memories I have!' The lines could end with an exclamation mark, if that were not too emphatic for the gentle movement: this father, finding he has a living child, not a slaughtered one, does not give vent to loud rejoicings, but quiet amazement. Nor, of course, does he give way to loud grief, as Hercules does. In mood it is much closer to that of the 'recognition' scene in *Pericles,* and 'Marina' echoes Pericles's bemused questioning of Marina – 'But are you flesh and blood? / Have you a working pulse ...?' (V.1.152–3) – when the poem *does* ask questions (with a question mark): 'What is this face ... / The pulse ... / Given or lent?'

Nature breathes and speaks here more prominently and positively than in any other of the poems. Eliot thought of himself as a classicist in literature, given to order and balance, reason and restraint; but Eliot's romantic side is given the freest rein in this most overt expression of love and emotion, and it is highly appropriate that this should largely operate, as with so much **Romantic** poetry, through images from the natural world.

American scenery, particularly the north-east coast of his childhood holidays, made a greater impression on Eliot than any other, and Casco Bay, Maine, lies behind the setting of this poem, with its sea and shore, grey rocks and granite islands, pinewood and woodthrush, all wrapped in a typical sea fog to very different effect from the city fog so dingily and drearily present in urban poems like 'The Love Song of J. Alfred Prufrock', 'Portrait of a Lady' and *The Waste Land.* This is particularly the case of 'the woodsong fog', where the song of the woodthrush is brilliantly associated with its habitat and combined into one epithet for the fog – one of many moments in the poem where things are conflated, dissolve and merge.

The animal images seem presented as a conflation of the Seven Deadly Sins: Anger and Envy (in the violent); Ambition and Pride (in the glittering); Sloth and Greed (in the pig-sty dwellers); and Lust (in the ecstatic). As Deadly Sins are orthodoxly supposed to do, they all result in death, a point given emphasis by the fourfold repetition of the formula 'Those who ... meaning / Death' and with 'Death' made even more emphatic each time by being placed resoundingly at the start of the line. Reservations are sometimes felt about the distinct tone of this 'Death' chant, but those ugly thumps are 'reduced' and lose their substance as they dissolve miraculously into the wavelike return of pine and woodthrush and fog.

Waves and returning are central to the poem, not only in themes and images but also in structure. The patterns of repetition with variation are finely handled throughout. The first lines recur at the end, but with subtle variations: for example, the woodthrush is now more poignantly 'calling' through the fog, not just 'singing'; the 'grey rocks' are omitted, and the islands are strengthened by 'granite'; paradoxically, the final plain 'My daughter' is more affecting than the more overtly emotional rhetoric of 'O my daughter', but the emotion needs that reduction of the original phrase to get its full increased force. Beginning and end are also echoed near the middle in 'breath of pine' – a magically sense-altering variation on 'scent of pine' – and 'woodsong fog', and further structural cohesion comes from the development of the boat imagery from the initial 'water lapping the bow', through the later series of references to the leaking old boat ('Bowsprit ... paint ... rigging ... canvas ... garboard strake ... seams') contrasted with 'the new ships', until the final 'my timbers' marvellously combines the language of boats with the references to wood in the pine, woodthrush and woodsong, and even 'leaves'. That last comes from a line ('Whispers and small laughter between leaves and hurrying feet') conveying the activities of children, and may at first be thought unrelated to the rest of the poem, but even this helps link up with the notion of remembering the past of children – children who are, highly appropriately, ghostly revenants, if we pick up the allusion to Kipling's story (see Commentaries). It is a lovely line, beautifully capturing quiet noises and scurrying, and it is not surprising that Eliot was to return to it again, with variations, in three places in his *Four Quartets*. In 'Marina', even more appropriately, given the poem's sense of waking after dreaming, and its maritime title and imagery, the line leads straight on to 'sleep, where all the waters meet': another resonant merging, in turn flowing on to the recollected boat, and likewise child, which the younger man made, forgot about, and remembers.

Just as the **rhythms** are wavelike, soothing and lulling, but never fixed, as where the 'Death' chant breaks into and then is broken down by the prevailing gentleness, so too the **rhymes** come and go. There are no end-rhymes for most of the poem, but they suddenly appear halfway through, with the sequence 'feet-meet-heat'; 'forgotten-remember-rotten-September' – and as suddenly disappear again. Even in this end-rhymed section, the rhythms and line lengths vary so much that the movement is unpredictable, the rhymes not coming in the expected places that would be given by a fixed number of **metrical** feet. Elsewhere, the rhymes are internal, where they appear at all, and this gives an even less fixed feel, as in 'grace dissolved in place // What is this face', where the three internal rhymes in the two lines reinforce the quality of dissolution marking the whole poem. Any fixed pattern of rhyme and rhythm would give a rigidity unsuitable for a poem of flux and reflux in which one thing is constantly dissolving into another. At the same time a prevailing tone is reflected in the prevailing gentle rhythms and unobtrusive rhymes: it is highly charged and evocative, but hushed and awestruck and reverent.

The liturgical note of all the other poems of this period is absent, but 'grace' is truly here: it is the only overtly religious word in the poem, but an extremely potent one. It always appears in Eliot's work in a religious context. In *Murder in the Cathedral* it appears twice in the phrase 'by God's grace', and in the ninth Chorus from *The Rock* is related to our duty to God: 'Shall we not bring to Your service all our powers / For life, for dignity, grace and order ...?' In the second part of *Burnt Norton* (1941), the first of Eliot's *Four Quartets*, the word appears in a religious meditation as 'a grace of sense, a white light'. But the clearest analogues are in *Ash-Wednesday*: the second part has 'Grace to the Mother' in its litany of prayer, and the fifth, with 'No place of grace for those who avoid the face' actually employs the identical three internal rhymes as 'Marina', as it too fuses grace and place, and envisages another blessed face. Further links between the two poems are provided by the powerful development in 'Marina' of the sea and ships imagery of the sixth and last part of *Ash-Wednesday*. Though the ship approaching the granite islands of the new world may be old and leaking, the victory over death is positive; even to 'Resign' life this time brings a totally positive anticipation of the new life, 'the hope, the new ships'. The images merge and regather in the overwhelming final cadences, until the breathed 'My daughter' fades out the sublime music. The least superficially religious poem of this period has become, at a deeper level, the most so.

Paternity is the theme of the poem, according to Eliot; it is clearly *one* theme, at any rate. (Can you come up with any other theme or themes? Some clues are given elsewhere in this analysis.) As in the Shakespearian and Senecan allusions, this theme is most affectingly treated. Eliot was not himself a father, but he has here imagined what it is like to be a father, and especially the emotions felt by a father for a daughter from whom he has been parted. It is very persuasively done, seeming to most readers very true to life. It is certainly one of the most powerful statements of paternal love ever written by a man who did not experience fatherhood personally. Do you think that adds to the emotional impact of the poem? Do you think it would make the poem more poignant still if it were revealed that Eliot did in fact have a daughter? Or do you think these are irrelevant or invalid considerations?

Fatherhood has to do with creation, and that is why it is so effective when the memory of creating the child merges with the memory of creating the boat. 'Between one June and another September' could mean succeeding summers when the boat was built, but 'another September', in suggesting a month in 'another' year, also gives nine months from a daughter's conception in September to her birth in June. Likewise, in its age and decrepitude the boat seems to be associated with its creator, who lets the old boat give way to the 'new ships' in the same way that he offers up his life for his daughter's.

Poetry is creation, too; and in poetry of this calibre Eliot will surely continue to be regarded as one of the great creative geniuses.

PART FIVE

Background

T. S. Eliot's Life

Thomas Stearns Eliot was born in St Louis, Missouri, an inland industrial city of America, on 26 September 1888. The future poet was the youngest of the seven children of a businessman and a school-mistress. His mother herself wrote poetry and was evidently a stimulating influence on her son, for whom she wished a literary success to compensate for her own lack of recognition. Eliot's mother also taught him to revere the example of his paternal grandfather, a pillar of respectability whom he never knew, but whose laws of self-denial and public service became deeply ingrained in his grandson. Inheriting his grandfather's missionary zeal and sense of duty, Eliot was well-equipped to bring a message to the inhabitants of modern Western civilisation, which he saw as a moral and cultural wasteland. The habit of self-denial, however, had its unhappy side: Eliot later admitted his resulting inability to enjoy many of the pleasures of life. Often, for instance, he treats sexual matters in his poems with a disgust plainly born of guilt and dissatisfaction.

There were, of course, pleasures in Eliot's life, and his childhood seems to have been a particularly enjoyable one. As many of the happiest summers were spent on the New England coast, it is not surprising that the sea speaks powerfully through his poetry at times of innocence recalled, awakening, or revelation. Indeed, sea themes and the language of sailing are prominent in the first of his writings to be published: his contributions to the magazine of Smith Academy, his school in St Louis, when he was sixteen.

A literary magazine at Harvard University, where Eliot began his studies in 1906, printed more early efforts of the young poet. It was not until 1915, however, that the earliest pieces in *Selected Poems* were published in periodicals, though these extraordinarily original works were written mainly in 1910–11, about the time Eliot took a year off from Harvard to live in Paris and study at the Sorbonne. In these years Eliot became fascinated with those images drawn from the squalor of modern city life that were to become part of his poetic trademark. In 1914 he returned to Europe to begin brief periods of study at the Universities of Marburg and, with the outbreak of the First World War, Oxford.

The year of publication of the first four poems in *Selected Poems*, 1915, also found Eliot settling in London and marrying Vivienne Haigh-Wood. The marriage was to be a difficult one, its course marked by the nervous breakdowns of both parties and the chronic illness of Vivienne. In 1933 Eliot at last legally separated from his wife, who spent the last years of her life in a mental home, where she died in 1947. The strains of this relationship were undoubtedly reflected in Eliot's work; but care must be taken in using such biographical information to interpret the poetry. For instance, it is no use ascribing to this marriage alone the 'mad', neurotic qualities of some of the poems: 'Prufrock', which an influential editor, the poet Harold Monro (1879–1932), described as 'absolutely insane', was written years before Eliot met his wife.

After the wedding, Eliot was a schoolmaster for a year and a half before becoming a clerk in a London bank in 1917. The same year he published his first volume of poems, *Prufrock and Other Observations*, and became assistant editor of *The Egoist*, a literary journal. During the eight years he worked in the bank he continued publishing poetry and also began making his reputation as a critic, founding in 1922 (with the aid of a wealthy patron) his own literary magazine, *The Criterion*, which he edited until 1939. In 1925 he left the bank to join the publishing firm now known as Faber and Faber as a director – a job more in keeping with his role as leading man of letters, but still very much in the Eliot family tradition of regular daily work that he dutifully kept up all his days.

1927 marks two conversions in Eliot's life: he abandoned his American citizenship to become a British subject, and he was baptised into the Anglican Church. As it is Eliot's religious development that has most bearing on the poems, it will be briefly considered here. Eliot's home background was staunchly Unitarian, that is, based on a belief in God as one person, not as the orthodox Trinity of Father, Son, and Holy Ghost. As taught to Eliot, whose grandfather had founded the Unitarian church in St Louis, Unitarianism called essentially for right behaviour rather than right doctrine; it was based on what was 'done' and 'not done' rather than on ideas of good and evil; and it was concerned with enlightened commonsense morality rather than mystical spirituality. As this sort of down-to-earth, rational religion did not satisfy Eliot's more fervid and emotional side, nor his need to submit to an orthodox theological dogma, he had drifted right away from the Church by his student days. Attacks on the Church and Christianity appear in 'The Hippopotamus' (1917) and 'Mr Eliot's Sunday Morning Service' (1918), but during the 1920s religion increasingly offered a means of dealing with Eliot's private problems. Anglo-Catholicism, the movement within the Church of England seeking to uphold the best aspects of the ancient Roman Church, increasingly appealed to him, until, in the year that he took on the nationality of his English ancestors, he also embraced their religion.

During the previous five years he had produced only the poems that make up *The Hollow Men* (1925). Now come the last of the *Selected Poems*, with their specifically Christian themes: two of the *Ariel* poems, 'Journey of the Magi' (1927) and 'A Song for Simeon' (1928); *Ash Wednesday* (1930); the Choruses from the Christian pageant-play, *The Rock* (1934). Even the other two *Ariel* poems in *Selected Poems*, 'Animula' (1929) and 'Marina' (1930), are essentially 'religious' poems, in that they are concerned with reverence, the soul, grace and revelation. By the end of *Selected Poems*, then, we have come a long way from the earlier satires and sordidness, though some critics have been at pains to show an overall unity in Eliot's total output, an evolving pattern of development that links these apparently opposed periods.

The later part of Eliot's life does not concern us here, and may be even more briefly summarised. Spiritual interests, prominent in the latter half of *Selected Poems*, reappear in Eliot's five poetic dramas, beginning with *Murder in the Cathedral* (1935), and the poems of religious meditation that grew into *Four Quartets* (1943). In 1948, the year he turned sixty, Eliot received the Order of Merit and the Nobel Prize for Literature. This public reward was followed by a private one in 1957, when his second marriage finally brought great personal happiness in the eight years before his death in London on 4 January 1965.

Eliot's is probably the leading name in the 'Modern Movement' that brought about a revolution in English literature between about 1910 and 1930 – roughly the period covered by *Selected Poems*. With Ezra Pound (1885–1972), a fellow American who championed the work of Eliot and many other experimental writers, Eliot launched a new type of poetry in English that effectively broke away from the poetic tradition of the previous age. This, established by the **Romantic** poets of the nineteenth century, was still being followed by the two Americans' English contemporaries – the 'Georgians' – whom they regarded as merely conventional users of worn-out poetic subjects (chiefly pastoral) and methods. Similar revolutions occurred at about the same time in all the arts, as the **Modernists** ' demolished all received definitions of what art is: witness, for example, the prose writings of James Joyce (1882–1941), the paintings of Pablo Picasso (1881–1973), the music of Igor Stravinsky (1882–1971).

Eliot's poetry fits into these wider contexts of **Modernism** very straightforwardly. Joyce's *Ulysses* was published in the same year (1922) as *The Waste Land,* but sections of it appeared earlier and Eliot was worried that he might have been unduly influenced by such things as Joyce's use of myth in a modern context, his dense allusiveness and his techniques for presenting the stream of consciousness of a character's internal musings without conventional punctuation. Picasso's experiments in painting dislocated conventional subjects by (for instance) using geometric shapes to represent the body and putting the eyes on the same side of the nose – a visual parallel of Eliot's dislocations in words; we have already seen how related developments in painting reflect Eliot's 'collage' technique. As for music, Stravinsky's *Rite of Spring* in 1913 startled audiences by its primitive rhythmic violence and repetitiveness, its harsh dissonances and other allegedly 'unmusical' effects: Eliot attended a performance of the ballet in 1921 and noted the way it metamorphosed, rather as in his own poetry, 'the motor horn, the rattle of machinery, the grind of wheels, the beating of iron and steel, the roar of the underground railway, and the other barbaric cries of modern life' ('London Letter', *The Dial,* October 1921, p. 453). How lasting the influence of such innovators will be cannot be assessed yet; it suffices that they all contrived to 'Make it New', in Pound's famous phrase.

Eliot was making it new before he met Pound, but his poetic practice agreed with Poundian principles, notably that the poetry of the new age should be 'harder and saner ... austere, direct, free from emotional slither' (*Literary Essays*, Faber and Faber, 1954, p. 12); that it should create new **rhythms** and images but express these in the language of living speech (Eliot's style, though frequently 'literary', is often conversational); that it should aim at concentration and the exact word rather than vague effusiveness; and that it should tackle any subject the poet found relevant to his own experience, no matter how allegedly 'unpoetic' by traditional standards of taste. Indeed, during those two 'golden' decades of Modernism, educated literary taste itself changed, a change in which Eliot's own criticism played a large part: a 'difficult' and 'unmusical' poet such as John Donne (1572–1631) could be favourably contrasted with Edmund Spenser (*c.*1552–99) or John Milton (1608–74); Gerard Manley Hopkins (1844–89), for all his 'eccentricity', could be regarded as a greater Victorian poet than Alfred, Lord Tennyson (1809–92). It must have seemed to many hostile readers that oddity and obscurity were necessary ingredients if any poetry was to be appreciated by the new formers of taste.

In his joking, self-mocking irony, his modern city themes, the juxtaposition of the ordinary and the extraordinary, even the construction of his verse, Eliot was influenced by certain nineteenth-century French '**Symbolist**' poets; he frequently acknowledged them as the teachers to whom he went as a young man for a kind of poetry that did not exist in English. From Charles Baudelaire (1821–67), for example, Eliot said he learnt the poetical possibilities 'of the more sordid aspects of the modern metropolis, of the possibility of fusion between the sordidly realistic and the phantasmagoric' ('What Dante Means to Me', *To Criticize the Critic*, p. 126), and to Jules Laforgue (1860–87) he said he owed 'more than to any one poet in any language' ('To Criticize the Critic', *To Criticize the Critic*, p. 22). Laforgue, an influential technical innovator, was a pioneer of *vers libre* – '**free verse**' or verse freed from conventional rigid forms, with their regular metres and **rhyme**-schemes. But as Eliot said, 'No verse is free for the man who wants to do a good job' ('The Music of Poetry', *On Poets and Poetry*, p. 37); and there is much freer verse than his own, which is closer to Laforgue's *vers impairs*, that is, odd or uneven verse, with varying numbers of syllables to the line, and (instead of no rhyme at all) occasional, irregularly placed rhymes. Laforgue also invented a type of dramatic **monologue** now known as the 'interior monologue', which Eliot used a number of times, as in the first two of his *Selected Poems*, where we look into the mind of a character 'thinking aloud'. Eliot further developed such Laforguian methods as the kind of ironic 'doubling', distancing, and self-mockery also noticed particularly in the first two poems, where a cynical pessimism is lightened by verbal antics, and the dramatised mind leaps about from topic to topic.

A much earlier poet, Dante (1265–1321), is an even more pervasive presence in Eliot's work. The great Italian meant more to him than even Shakespeare, whom he thought more varied than Dante, with a greater breadth of humanity, but not so understanding of the heights and depths, 'deeper degrees of degradation and higher degrees of exaltation' ('Dante', *Selected Essays*, p. 252). He regarded Dante's poetry as 'the most persistent and deepest influence upon my own verse' ('What Dante Means to Me', *To Criticize the Critic*, p. 125) – a comment that can be set against his remark on Laforgue quoted above: Laforgue is an early influence, Dante a lasting one. The presence of Dante in *Selected Poems* ranges from the quotation used as the **epigraph** or motto at the head of the first poem, through allusions in *The Waste Land* and inserted English imitations of Dante such as the first line of 'Animula', to the large-scale adaptation of Dantean themes and patterns of imagery in *Ash-Wednesday*. No simple listing of allusions can properly illustrate that sort of 'borrowing', encompassing Dante's Christian beliefs, attempting the simple beauty of his language, extending the range of his **symbols**, recreating the whole 'feel' of his verse. But at some stage you may wish to consult his *Divine Comedy* (*Divina Commedia*), a long poem in three books, in which Dante is taken by the spirit of the Roman poet Virgil (70–19BC) on a visit to the damned in Hell (*Inferno*); the waiting sufferers in intermediate Purgatory (*Purgatorio*); and the blessed souls in Paradise (*Paradiso*). Eliot also drew on an earlier work of Dante's, his *New Life* (*Vita Nuova*), a preparation for the *Comedy*, introducing the poet's love for Beatrice, in whom he sees his hope of being spiritually saved; Beatrice reappears to take over from Virgil as Dante's guide in the ascent from Purgatory to Paradise. She seems associated with Eliot's 'Lady' in *Ash-Wednesday*, developing the Dantean links with the Virgin Mary. On the other hand, in earlier poems like *The Waste Land* Eliot borrowed from Dante's *Hell*, to establish what he described as 'a relationship between the medieval inferno and modern life' (*To Criticize the Critic*, p. 128).

Modern life itself has contributed to Eliot's poetry. In an age of rapid change that has seen the collapse of traditional beliefs about the universe and about man himself, with scientific and technological advancement going hand in hand with a loss of spiritual and moral certainty; an age of breakdown and disorder; an age of migrations, political movements and conflicts on an unprecedentedly global scale; an age in which knowledge has increased so hugely that no one person can come to grips with more than sections of it – in the face of all this Eliot believed a true poetic response to the confusion must necessarily be difficult:

> Our civilisation comprehends great variety and complexity, and this variety and complexity, playing upon a refined sensibility, must produce various and complex results. The poet must become more and more comprehensive, more allusive, more indirect, in order to force, to dislocate if necessary, language into his meaning.

That quotation comes from Eliot's essay 'The Metaphysical Poets' (*Selected Essays*, p. 289), and it is no accident that he seemed to consider poets like Donne to be closer in spirit to himself than most other English poets of the intervening two centuries. Donne's reaction to the seventeenth century, which has been described as 'the fullest record in our literature of the disintegrating collision in a sensitive mind of the old tradition and the new learning', has similarities with Eliot's reaction to related developments in the twentieth century. Certainly the two poets share similar techniques, from their colloquial styles and vocabularies combining everyday words with unusual, 'bookish' ones, to their complex sentences mirroring complex feelings and their unexpected juxtapositions, which demand intelligence and speed of thought in their readers. Even when Eliot is critical of Donne, he could be (rather harshly) describing himself, as when he writes that the seventeenth-century world 'was filled with broken fragments of systems, and that a man like Donne merely picked up, like a magpie, various shining fragments of ideas as they struck his eye, and stuck them about here and there in his verse' ('Shakespeare and the Stoicism of Seneca', *Selected Essays*, pp. 138–9). For Eliot's is also a fragmentary response to a fragmented age. Only late in his career, with the help of his classicism, his conservatism and his orthodox Christian belief, did he approach an inclusive, controlled vision.

PART SIX

CRITICAL HISTORY & FURTHER READING

EARLY RECEPTION

A title such as *Storm over The Waste Land*, for a collection of essays edited by Robert E. Knoll (Scott Foresman, 1964), reminds us that from the first there were extremely hostile critical responses to Eliot, and especially to *The Waste Land*, which is widely seen as not only the most famous and admired but also the most notorious and abused poem of the twentieth century, the most influential but also the most resisted. Eliot is certainly a controversial poet. But we need to get the balance right, paradoxically, by recognising that the two sides are not really evenly balanced: the avalanche of positive commentary on Eliot far outweighs the mainly early attacks. And even from very early on there were always voices as loud in praise as in condemnation: Arthur Waugh (1866–1943) might describe 'The New Poetry' as 'drunken' ravings and 'unmetrical, incoherent banalities' as early as October 1916 (*Quarterly Review*, 226, p. 386), but equally, even before *The Waste Land* appeared, Clive Bell (1881–1964) represented the younger generation by hailing Eliot as 'the best of our living poets' (*The New Republic*, 28, 21 September 1921, p. 94). An air of baffled dismay was at first evinced by the more sympathetic critics as well as those traditional ones whose puzzlement led to violent antipathy. Very quickly, however, both sides came to see Eliot as an unignorable feature of the literary landscape: as George Watson expresses it in 'The Triumph of T.S. Eliot', 'admirers and detractors were equally agreed about the reality of his reputation' (*Critical Quarterly*, 7, Winter 1965, p. 329).

- Apart from the two volumes of Michael Grant, ed., *The Critical Heritage*, Routledge & Kegan Paul, 1982, with a comprehensive collection of reviews of Eliot's poetry and plays at the time of their publication, see the four volumes of Graham Clarke, ed., *T.S. Eliot: Critical Assessments*, Christopher Helm, 1990, which ranges from 1916 to 1988.

A great poet creates the taste by which he is appreciated, but when that poet is also a great critic then the process is made even easier: in playing such a large part in shaping the history of literary criticism in the first half of the twentieth century, Eliot certainly helped his reputation as a poet as well as a critic. The New Criticism, dominant from the 1930s to the 1960s in Britain and especially America, was largely a response to the new poetry of Eliot, Pound and Yeats, and followed Eliot's recommendation that a poem should be studied as something 'autotelic', that is, as a self-sufficient verbal artefact and not as biography or sociology or history or psychology or anything extrinsic to the poetry itself. Apart from the poet-critic's own critical principles and practice, the greatest impetus was given by I.A. Richards (1893–1979), whose *Principles of Literary Criticism* (Kegan Paul, Trench, Trubner, 1924), with an appendix on Eliot's poetry in the 1926 reissue, was hailed by Eliot as changing the course of literary criticism and even altering the meaning of the term, and whose *Practical Criticism* (Kegan Paul, Trench, Trubner, 1929) virtually gave birth to the New Criticism. Two of Richards's students at Cambridge, William Empson (1906–84) and F.R. Leavis, helped in extending Eliot's reputation by featuring his poetry in highly influential books of criticism employing what were to become the favoured New Critical methods of keeping to the 'words on the page' and subjecting them to 'close reading': Empson's *Seven Types of Ambiguity* (Chatto and Windus, 1930) and Leavis's *New Bearings in English Poetry* (Chatto and Windus, 1932). While all these critics – Eliot, Richards, Empson, Leavis – may be said to have helped establish the New Criticism, most of the 'New Critics' themselves were American: among those associated with the movement who wrote about Eliot were, in alphabetical order:

- R.P. Blackmur (1904–65), considered by Eliot and others to be the best close reader of modern poetry, as in the collection of his essays – two of them on Eliot – entitled *Language as Gesture* (George Allen & Unwin, 1954);
- Cleanth Brooks (1906–90), whose *Modern Poetry and the Tradition* (University of North Carolina Press, 1939) put Eliot in a tradition stemming from the metaphysical poets of the seventeenth century;
- John Crowe Ransom (1888–1974), whose *The New Criticism* (New Directions, 1941) gave currency to the name of the movement; and

• Allen Tate (1899–1979), whose edited symposium on *T.S. Eliot: The Man and His Work* (Chatto and Windus, 1967) is still useful.

An American study previously cited, with a pioneering chapter on Eliot, is independent of this grouping:
• Edmund Wilson, *Axel's Castle* (Charles Scribner's Sons, 1931), tracing the origins of the **Modernist** movement.

LATER CRITICAL HISTORY

The New Criticism ensured that Eliot's reputation rode high over several decades, with some falling off in the 1950s, when the poetry of the 'Movement' led to attempts to displace Modernism by championing a rival 'native' English tradition from Thomas Hardy to Philip Larkin, while in America Eliot's kind of Modernism was downgraded: in both countries, poetic practice markedly abandoned Eliot's techniques. Literary studies, however, did not fail to continue to give Eliot a high profile, which still continues.

Two excellent *short introductions* to Eliot are:
• M.C. Bradbrook, *T.S. Eliot*, Longman, 1965
• Northrop Frye, *T.S. Eliot*, Oliver and Boyd, 1963

Longer general accounts of varying usefulness include:
• Bernard Bergonzi, *T.S. Eliot*, 2nd edn, Macmillan, 1978
• Ronald Bush, *T.S. Eliot: A Study in Character and Style*, Oxford University Press,1983
• Angus Calder, *T.S. Eliot*, Harvester, 1987
• Helen Gardner, *The Art of T.S. Eliot*, Cresset Press, 1949
• Piers Gray, *T.S. Eliot's Intellectual and Poetic Development 1909–1922*, Harvester, 1982
• Hugh Kenner, *The Invisible Poet: T.S. Eliot*, W.H. Allen, 1960
• F.O. Matthiessen, *The Achievement of T.S. Eliot*, 3rd edn, enlarged by C.L. Barber, Oxford University Press, 1958
• Louis Menand, *Discovering Modernism: T.S. Eliot and His Context*, Oxford University Press, 1987

- A.D. Moody, *Thomas Stearns Eliot: Poet*, Cambridge University Press, 1979
- Martin Scofield, *T.S. Eliot: The Poems*, Cambridge University Press, 1988
- Stephen Spender, *Eliot*, Fontana, 1975
- C.K. Stead, *The New Poetic: Yeats to Eliot*, Hutchinson, 1964
- Ronald Tamplin, *A Preface to T.S. Eliot*, Longman, 1987
- George Williamson, *A Reader's Guide to T.S. Eliot*, enlarged edn, Thames and Hudson, 1967

SOME SPECIAL TYPES OF RECENT STUDY

Biographical studies have given new interest in a poet who was anxious to exclude them and requested that no biography of him should be written. Of these, Peter Ackroyd's lively *T.S. Eliot* (Hamish Hamilton, 1984) has been found most persuasive in conveying Eliot's personality, while the best in linking the life and the works in a sensitive yet detailed scholarly manner is Lyndall Gordon's beautifully written *T.S. Eliot* (Vintage, 1998), combining her *Eliot's Early Years* and *Eliot's New Life* (Oxford University Press, 1977 and 1988).

Sources of Eliot's poetry have been treated in detail in relation to meaning in Grover Smith's exhaustive *T.S. Eliot's Poetry and Plays* (University of Chicago Press, revised edition, 1974) and B.C. Southam's handy *A Student's Guide to the Selected Poems of T.S. Eliot* (Faber and Faber, fourth edition, 1981).

Specialist studies abound. *Feminist* studies are still surprisingly thin on the ground, but Eliot's treatment of women has come in for much attention by critics of various critical persuasions, notably the *psychoanalytic*, as in Tony Pinkney's *Women in the Poetry of T.S. Eliot: A Psychoanalytic Approach* (Macmillan, 1984). An interesting *anthropological* approach is Robert Crawford's *The Savage and the City in the Work of T.S. Eliot* (Clarendon Press, 1987), while Eliot's anti-semitism (and much else) has been alertly explored by Christopher Ricks in *T.S. Eliot and Prejudice* (Faber and Faber, 1988).

Introducing the four volumes of *T.S. Eliot: Critical Assessments* (Christopher Helm, 1990), Graham Clarke remarks on the 'continuous and ever-enlarging response' to a body of work that 'remains consistently problematic and tendentious': 'while there might be a consensus regarding Eliot's *status*, the terms on which the work is gauged, discussed and "explained" remain diffuse, questioning and, in some instances, diffident and antagonistic' (p. 1). As the critical debate surrounding Eliot's poetic achievement is likely to go on for a good while yet, some of the points continuing to be at issue may be helpful in concluding the broader perspectives.

Because of its frequent obscurity, its learnedness, its quotations and allusions, Eliot's poetry often seems to be deliberately elitist, seeking to appeal to an intellectual minority rather than a wide audience. But Eliot himself said this:

> I believe that the poet naturally prefers to write for as large and miscellaneous an audience as possible, and that it is the half-educated and ill-educated, rather than the uneducated, who stand in his way: I myself should like an audience which could neither read nor write.

This remark, from the conclusion to *The Use of Poetry and the Use of Criticism* (p. 152), could hardly be further from a desire for a limited and highly literate audience of adepts. So, while it is true that Eliot is not a popular poet in the sense that he is read by a mass audience (more have heard of *The Waste Land* than actually read it), the comparative smallness of his public may say more about his reputation as a 'difficult' poet than about his potential appeal. And perhaps one should stress that 'comparative': by the standards of most poets, Eliot is read very widely indeed, as the unflagging reprintings of his works testify.

A reputation for intellectual difficulty – and it is pointless to deny a measure of difficulty in Eliot – is not the only block to a (still) wider appeal. Criticism has also been levelled at the narrowness of Eliot's interests, and particularly to a gap in his poetry that has been neatly summed up by Grover Smith, who regretted that Eliot's poetry 'shows no Beatrice' (*T.S. Eliot's Poetry and Plays*, University of Chicago Press, revised edition, 1974, p. 7): certainly women in his work are remote or idealised or unsexual or disgusting or predatory or hysterical or frightening – almost anything, it seems, except being seen as receiving 'normal' sexual love and affection. The few presentations of positive love do not alter this general truth: the 'hyacinth girl' in *The Waste Land* brings pain rather than pleasure; love in 'Marina' is for a daughter. This leads to the related objection that there is so much that is negative in this poetry, so much rejection, sterility and renunciation.

But such views, even if we share them, must not blind us to the virtues of the poetry *as poetry*, whatever the subject matter; nor must any intellectual emphasis, or Eliot's rejection of certain romantic attitudes, or his protective mask of irony, be allowed to oust from our minds a realisation of the fundamentally emotional nature of this poetry. It betrays the romantic side of the poet's temperament and the depths of feeling from which, with a voice controlled by a critical intelligence, he speaks most powerfully and memorably. As his readers, we owe these kinds of recognition to Eliot if we are to be responsible in our responsiveness.

'A thorough knowledge of Eliot is compulsory for anyone interested in contemporary literature. Whether he is liked or disliked is of no importance, but he must be read.' Northrop Frye's words in his *T.S. Eliot* (Oliver and Boyd, 1963, p. 5) are still true, though some would wish to stress that the sense of the importance of the poetry does not rule out enjoyment and excitement. The excitement was still there for Ezra Pound after his friend's death, in 'For TSE', written for Allen Tate, ed., *T.S. Eliot: The Man and His Work* (Chatto and Windus, 1967, p. 92): 'I can only repeat, but with the urgency of fifty years ago: READ HIM.'

CHRONOLOGY

World events	T.S. Eliot's life	Literary & artistic events
		1857 Charles Baudelaire, *Fleurs du Mal*
1861 Southern States of USA secede from Union; American Civil War begins		
1865 End of American Civil War		
1870-1 Franco-Prussian War		
		1874 Thomas Hardy, *Far From the Madding Crowd*
		1885 Jule Laforgue, *Les Complaintes*
1887 Queen Victoria's Golden Jubilee		
	1888 T.S. Eliot born 26 September, St Louis, Missouri	
		1893 W.B. Yeats, *The Lake Isle of Innisfree*
		1895 Thomas Hardy, *Jude the Obscure*
		1898 Thomas Hardy, *Wessex Poems*
1899-1902 Boer War		
1901 Death of Queen Victoria		**1901** Pablo Picasso, *Blue Room;* Thomas Hardy, *Poems of the Past and Present*
	1906 Begins studies at Harvard	
		1909 Ezra Pound, *Personae*
1910 Death of Edward VII	**1910-11** Writes earliest poems; leaves Harvard to study in Paris for a year	**1910** Igor Stravinsky, *The Firebird*
		1912 Pablo Picasso, *Still Life with Chair*
		1913 Igor Stravinsky, *The Rite of Spring*
1914-18 First World War	**1914** Returns to Europe to study at Marburg and Oxford	**1914** James Joyce, *Dubliners;* W.B. Yeats, *Responsibilities;* Thomas Hardy, *Satires of Circumstance*

World events	T.S. Eliot's life	Literary & artistic events
	1915 Earliest poems published in periodicals; settles in London; marries Vivienne Haigh-Wood; becomes schoolmaster	
		1916 James Joyce, *A Portait of the Artist as a Young Man*
	1917 Becomes bank clerk in London; publishes *Prufrock and Other Observations*; becomes assistant editor of *The Egoist*	**1917** Thomas Hardy, *Moments of Vision*
	1920 *The Sacred Wood*	
	1922 *The Waste Land*; founds *The Criterion*	**1922** James Joyce, *Ulysses*; Thomas Hardy, *Late Lyrics and Earlier*
1924 Labour Party takes office for first time		
	1925 Joins Faber and Faber as a director; *The Hollow Men*	**1925** Ezra Pound, *Cantos*; W.B. Yeats, *A Vision*
1926 General Strike		
	1927 Becomes British subject; baptised into Anglican Church; *Journey of the Magi*	
	1928 *A Song for Simeon; For Lancelot Andrewes*	**1928** W.B. Yeats, *The Tower*; Thomas Hardy, *Winter Words*
1929 Collapse of New York stock exchange heralds world depression		
	1930 *Ash-Wednesday; Marina*	
	1932 *Sweeney Agonistes*	
1933 Hitler appointed Chancellor in Germany	**1933** Legally separates from Vivienne	**1933** D.H. Lawrence, *Last Poems*
	1934 *The Rock*	
	1935 *Murder in the Cathedral*	

CHRONOLOGY

World events	T.S. Eliot's life	Literary & artistic events
1936 Death of George V; abdication of Edward VIII		**1936** Dylan Thomas, *Twenty-five Poems*
		1937 Pablo Picasso, *Guernica;* Stevie Smith, *A Good Time Was Had by All*
1939-45 Second World War	**1939** *The Family Reunion*	**1939** James Joyce, *Finnegans Wake*
	1940 *The Idea of a Christian Society*	
	1943 *Four Quartets*	
1946 National Health Act provides free health care to all		
	1947 Vivienne dies in a mental home	
	1948 Receives Order of Merit and Nobel Prize for Literature; *Notes Towards the Definition of Culture*	
	1949 *The Cocktail Party*	
		1950 Ezra Pound, *Collected Poems*
		1951 Igor Stravinsky, *The Rake's Progress*
1952 Death of George VI		**1952** Samuel Beckett, *Waiting for Godot;* Philip Larkin, *The Less Deceived*
	1954 *The Confidential Clerk*	
	1957 Remarries	**1957** Ted Hughes, *The Hawk in the Rain;* Stevie Smith, *Not Waving but Drowning*
	1958 *The Elder Statesman*	
1960 Macmillan makes 'Wind of Change' speech		**1960** Sylvia Plath, *The Colossus*
1961 Berlin Wall built		
1963 President Kennedy assassinated		
		1964 Philip Larkin, *The Whitsun Weddings*
	1965 Dies 4 January	

(This list does not include terms made clear in their context above, or sufficiently defined in any good English dictionary)

alliteration the repetition of consonantal sounds (usually at the beginning of a word, and often in successive words) in a piece of writing

anticlimax, or **bathos** a ludicrous descent (intentional or unintentional) from the elevated or dramatic to the mundane or ordinary

assonance the use of the same vowel sounds with different consonants in successive words or stressed syllables e.g. nation and traitor

blank verse unrhymed iambic pentameters, lines of five iambs, which have a weak followed by a strong stress

epigraph the quotation(s) placed at the beginning of some sections of literary works to act as a kind of motto, or an indicator of the meaning

free verse verse released from the convention of metre with its regular pattern of stresses and lengths. It is printed in broken-up lines like verse (not continuously like prose) and is often very rhythmical

metaphor a figure of speech in which a word or phrase is applied to an object or action that it does not literally denote in order to imply a resemblance

metrical of metre and metrics, using patterns of stresses, a feature of poetry that distinguishes it from prose

mock-heroic a term applied to the style of a work that treats a 'low' or trivial subject in a 'high' or grand style, the inflatedness of manner thereby ridiculing the matter

Modernist applied to the innovative, experimental, revolutionary writers and other artists most prominent in the period from about 1910 to 1930

monologue spoken by a single person, with or without an audience. A **dramatic monologue** is a type of poem in which a dramatised character, to be distinguished from the poet himself, is speaking; **interior monologue** attempts to convey a character's internal consciousness or thought

onomatopoeia a Greek word meaning 'name-making', by which poets use words that sound like the things being described, in their action, movement, appearance or (especially) noise

pathos a Greek word meaning 'suffering', used of moments in literature that evoke feelings of pity and sadness

prolepsis a Greek word meaning 'anticipation', referring to a description that is used in advance of its appropriate application, in an anachronistic or prophetic way, as in Hamlet's 'I am dead, Horatio'

quatrain a stanza of four lines, frequently rhymed a-b-a-b or a-b-c-b

rhyme chiming or matching sounds which create a very clearly audible sense of pattern

rhythm the chief element of rhythm is the variation in levels of stress accorded to the syllables

Romantic wide-ranging term to describe the literary movement dominating the period roughly from 1789 to 1830, in which the principal English poets were Wordsworth, Coleridge, Byron, Keats and Shelley. Among the chief attributes is a valuing of feeling and emotion above logic and reason

simile a figure of speech in which one thing is explicitly said to be like another; similes always contain the words 'like' or 'as'

Symbolism use of symbols by any writers or other artists, but in particular those influenced (as Eliot was) by the French Symbolist poets of the nineteenth century

symbols things that represent other things, as Christianity may be represented by a cross, or purity by a lily; a writer like Eliot not only uses conventional symbols like these, but also invents his own

versification the art of writing metrically, as used in composing verse

AUTHOR OF THIS NOTE

Dr Michael Herbert was educated at the Universities of Cape Town, London and Oxford before taking up a lectureship in English at the University of St Andrews, where he specialises in English literature of the twentieth century. He has published critical works on various modern writers, including editions of D. H. Lawrence's essays (Cambridge, 1988) and critical writings (Oxford, 1998).

York Notes Advanced

Margaret Atwood
Cat's Eye

Margaret Atwood
The Handmaid's Tale

Jane Austen
Mansfield Park

Jane Austen
Persuasion

Jane Austen
Pride and Prejudice

Alan Bennett
Talking Heads

William Blake
Songs of Innocence and of Experience

Charlotte Brontë
Jane Eyre

Emily Brontë
Wuthering Heights

Angela Carter
Nights at the Circus

Geoffrey Chaucer
The Franklin's Tale

Geoffrey Chaucer
The Miller's Prologue and Tales

Geoffrey Chaucer
Prologue To the Canterbury Tales

Geoffrey Chaucer
The Wife of Bath's Prologue and Tale

Joseph Conrad
Heart of Darkness

Charles Dickens
Great Expectations

Charles Dickens
Hard Times

Emily Dickinson
Selected Poems

John Donne
Selected Poems

Carol Ann Duffy
Selected Poems

George Eliot
Middlemarch

George Eliot
The Mill on the Floss

T.S. Eliot
Selected Poems

F. Scott Fitzgerald
The Great Gatsby

E.M. Forster
A Passage to India

Brian Friel
Translations

Thomas Hardy
The Mayor of Casterbridge

Thomas Hardy
The Return of the Native

Thomas Hardy
Selected Poems

Thomas Hardy
Tess of the d'Urbervilles

Seamus Heaney
Selected Poems from Opened Ground

Nathaniel Hawthorne
The Scarlet Letter

Kazou Ishiguru
The Remains of the Day

James Joyce
Dubliners

John Keats
Selected Poems

Christopher Marlowe
Doctor Faustus

Arthur Miller
Death of a Salesman

John Milton
Paradise Lost Books I & II

Toni Morrison
Beloved

William Shakespeare
Antony and Cleopatra

William Shakespeare
As You Like It

William Shakespeare
Hamlet

William Shakespeare
King Lear

William Shakespeare
Measure for Measure

William Shakespeare
The Merchant of Venice

William Shakespeare
A Midsummer Night's Dream

William Shakespeare
Much Ado About Nothing

William Shakespeare
Othello

William Shakespeare
Richard II

William Shakespeare
Romeo and Juliet

William Shakespeare
The Taming of the Shrew

William Shakespeare
The Tempest

William Shakespeare
The Winter's Tale

George Bernard Shaw
Saint Joan

Mary Shelley
Frankenstein

Alice Walker
The Color Purple

Oscar Wilde
The Importance of Being Earnest

Tennessee Williams
A Streetcar Named Desire

John Webster
The Duchess of Malfi

Virginia Woolf
To the Lighthouse

W.B. Yeats
Selected Poems

OTHER TITLES

GCSE and equivalent levels

Maya Angelou
I Know Why the Caged Bird Sings

Jane Austen
Pride and Prejudice

Alan Ayckbourn
Absent Friends

Elizabeth Barrett Browning
Selected Poems

Robert Bolt
A Man for All Seasons

Harold Brighouse
Hobson's Choice

Charlotte Brontë
Jane Eyre

Emily Brontë
Wuthering Heights

Shelagh Delaney
A Taste of Honey

Charles Dickens
David Copperfield

Charles Dickens
Great Expectations

Charles Dickens
Hard Times

Charles Dickens
Oliver Twist

Roddy Doyle
Paddy Clarke Ha Ha Ha

George Eliot
Silas Marner

George Eliot
The Mill on the Floss

William Golding
Lord of the Flies

Oliver Goldsmith
She Stoops To Conquer

Willis Hall
The Long and the Short and the Tall

Thomas Hardy
Far from the Madding Crowd

Thomas Hardy
The Mayor of Casterbridge

Thomas Hardy
Tess of the d'Urbervilles

Thomas Hardy
The Withered Arm and other Wessex Tales

L.P. Hartley
The Go-Between

Seamus Heaney
Selected Poems

Susan Hill
I'm the King of the Castle

Barry Hines
A Kestrel for a Knave

Louise Lawrence
Children of the Dust

Harper Lee
To Kill a Mockingbird

Laurie Lee
Cider with Rosie

Arthur Miller
The Crucible

Arthur Miller
A View from the Bridge

Robert O'Brien
Z for Zachariah

Frank O'Connor
My Oedipus Complex and other stories

George Orwell
Animal Farm

J.B. Priestley
An Inspector Calls

Willy Russell
Educating Rita

Willy Russell
Our Day Out

J.D. Salinger
The Catcher in the Rye

William Shakespeare
Henry IV Part 1

William Shakespeare
Henry V

William Shakespeare
Julius Caesar

William Shakespeare
Macbeth

William Shakespeare
The Merchant of Venice

William Shakespeare
A Midsummer Night's Dream

William Shakespeare
Much Ado About Nothing

William Shakespeare
Romeo and Juliet

William Shakespeare
The Tempest

William Shakespeare
Twelfth Night

George Bernard Shaw
Pygmalion

Mary Shelley
Frankenstein

R.C. Sherriff
Journey's End

Rukshana Smith
Salt on the snow

John Steinbeck
Of Mice and Men

Robert Louis Stevenson
Dr Jekyll and Mr Hyde

Jonathan Swift
Gulliver's Travels

Robert Swindells
Daz 4 Zoe

Mildred D. Taylor
Roll of Thunder, Hear My Cry

Mark Twain
Huckleberry Finn

James Watson
Talking in Whispers

William Wordsworth
Selected Poems

A Choice of Poets

Mystery Stories of the Nineteenth Century including The Signalman

Nineteenth Century Short Stories

Poetry of the First World War

Six Women Poets

Chinua Achebe
Things Fall Apart

Edward Albee
Who's Afraid of Virginia Woolf?

Jane Austen
Emma

Jane Austen
Northanger Abbey

Jane Austen
Sense and Sensibility

Samuel Beckett
Waiting for Godot and *Endgame*

Louis de Bernières
Captain Corelli's Mandolin

Charlotte Brontë
Villette

Robert Browning
Selected Poems

Robert Burns
Selected Poems

Geoffrey Chaucer
The Merchant's Tale

Geoffrey Chaucer
The Nun's Priest's Tale

Caryl Churchill
Top Girls and *Cloud Nine*

Samuel Taylor Coleridge
Selected Poems

Daniel Defoe
Moll Flanders

Daniel Defoe
Robinson Crusoe

Charles Dickens
Bleak House

T.S. Eliot
The Waste Land

Henry Fielding
Joseph Andrews

E.M. Forster
Howards End

John Fowles
The French Lieutenant's Woman

Anne Frank
The Diary of Anne Frank

Robert Frost
Selected Poems

Elizabeth Gaskell
North and South

Stella Gibbons
Cold Comfort Farm

Graham Greene
Brighton Rock

Thomas Hardy
Jude the Obscure

Joseph Heller
Catch-22

Homer
The Iliad

Homer
The Odyssey

Gerard Manley Hopkins
Selected Poems

Henrik Ibsen
The Doll's House and *Ghosts*

Ben Jonson
The Alchemist

Ben Jonson
Volpone

James Joyce
A Portrait of the Artist as a Young Man

Philip Larkin
Selected Poems

Aldous Huxley
Brave New World

D.H. Lawrence
The Rainbow

D.H. Lawrence
Selected Poems

D.H. Lawrence
Selected Stories

D.H. Lawrence
Sons and Lovers

D.H. Lawrence
Women in Love

Christopher Marlowe
Edward II

John Milton
Paradise Lost Bks IV & IX

Thomas More
Utopia

Sean O'Casey
Juno and the Paycock

George Orwell
Nineteen Eighty-four

John Osborne
Look Back in Anger

Wilfred Owen
Selected Poems

Sylvia Plath
Selected Poems

Alexander Pope
Rape of the Lock and other poems

Ruth Prawer Jhabvala
Heat and Dust

J.B. Priestley
When We Are Married

Jean Rhys
Wide Sargasso Sea

William Shakespeare
As You Like It

William Shakespeare
Coriolanus

William Shakespeare
Henry IV Pt I

Wliiam Shakespeare
Henry IV Part II

William Shakespeare
Henry V

William Shakespeare
Julius Caesar

William Shakespeare
Macbeth

William Shakespeare
Measure for Measure

William Shakespeare
Richard III

William Shakespeare
Sonnets

William Shakespeare
Twelfth Night

William Shakespeare
The Winter's Tale

George Bernard Shaw
Arms and the Man

Muriel Spark
The Prime of Miss Jean Brodie

John Steinbeck
The Grapes of Wrath

John Steinbeck
The Pearl

Tom Stoppard
Arcadia and *Rosencrantz and Guildenstern are Dead*

Jonathan Swift
Gulliver's Travels and The Modest Proposal

Alfred, Lord Tennyson
Selected Poems

W.M. Thackeray
Vanity Fair

Virgil
The Aeneid

Edith Wharton
Ethan Frome

Jeanette Winterson
Oranges are Not the Only Fruit and *Written on the Body*

Tennessee Williams
Cat on a Hot Tin Roof

Tennessee Williams
The Glass Menagerie

Virginia Woolf
Mrs Dalloway

William Wordsworth
Selected Poems

The Diary of Anne Frank

Metaphysical Poets